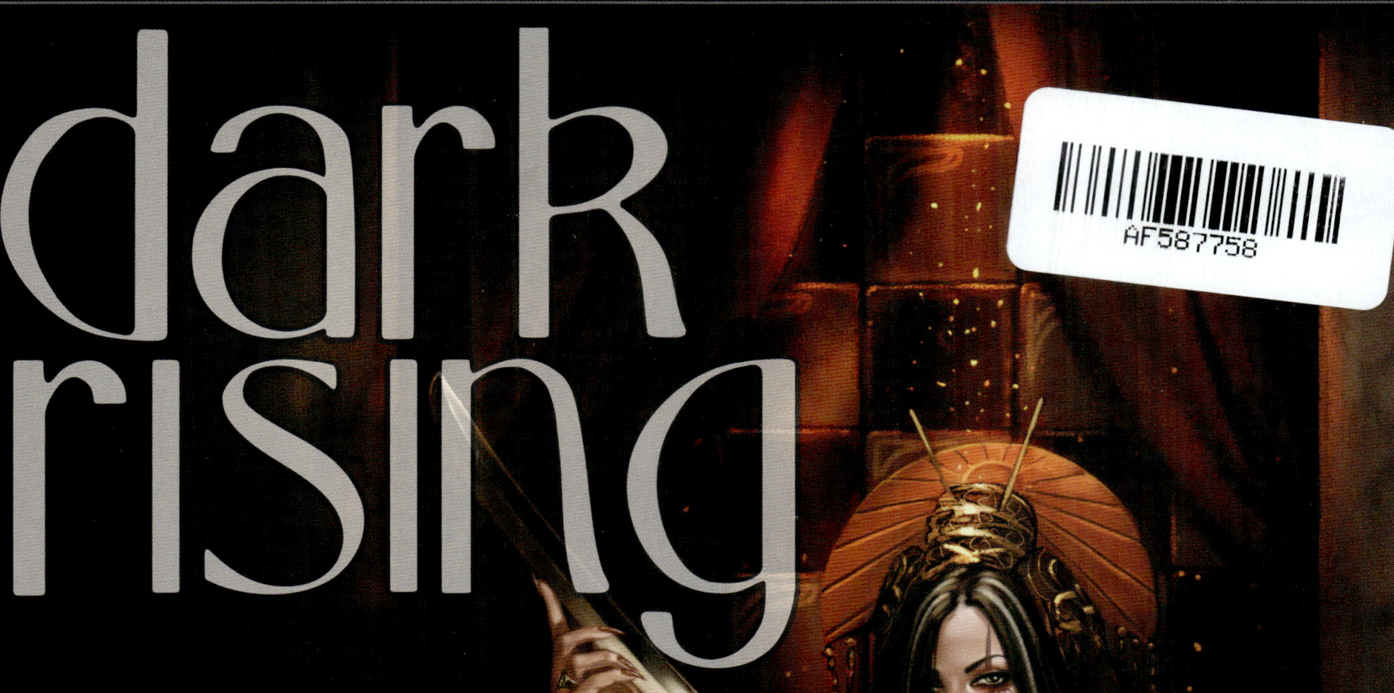

dark rising

THE ART OF ALY FELL

AN SQP PRESENTATION

DARK RISINGS *Pin-Ups with a Purpose...*

It's funny. If you paint women, and specifically women, you get called a 'pin-up' artist. I'm not entirely sure I'm worthy of that title... I like painting women, almost exclusively, but I prefer to think it's really women 'doing stuff'. Not always; I've done my fair share of work that pastiches wonderful artists such a Gil Elvgren or Joe Chiodo, whom I admire enormously. But I always come back to what I like doing... and that's... women doing stuff! Or if they're not 'doing stuff', at least it looks like there's a back story; that they have just done something interesting, or are poised to do so. I like a bit of cleavage; but their personality, clothes and history appeal far more, and to be honest I find all of that much more exciting, creatively. At a convention recently a woman remarked: "You draw women I want to be, rather than women I feel I ought to be." That was just what I wanted to hear, and I said so. She smiled, I smiled. She bought a print!

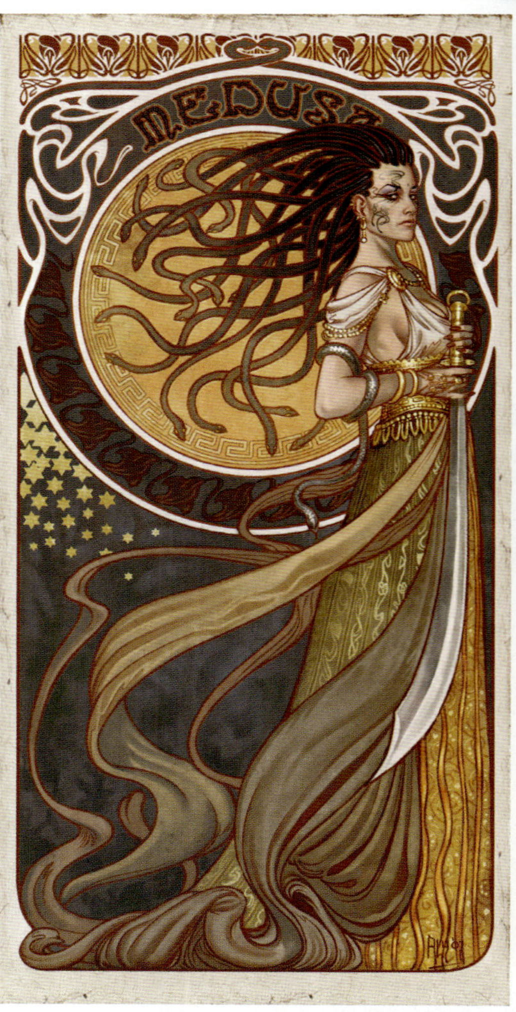

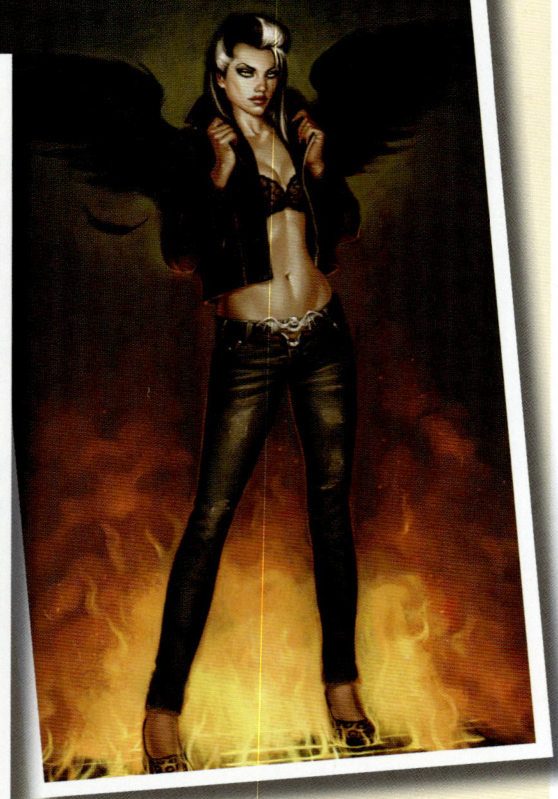

Left: Medusa Right: Elle Hellbound

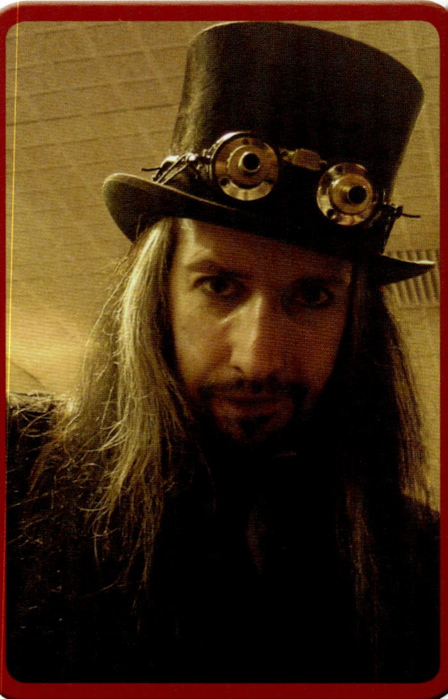

Aly Fell is a self-employed UK based illustrator, working out of a Manchester attic, where if he changes his spectacles, can just see some trees from his skylight. Previously a traditional 2D animator, Aly has also worked in the games industry, television, and edited art collections. He has an erratic web-comic: ***Rosie Poe***, and is currently working on a graphic novel set in Elizabethan England. He likes to wear far too much black and once drove a hearse as an everyday car... he likes cats, leather, pointy shoes and Twiglets, although not necessarily at the same time. His favourite film is ***'The Great Escape'***, so don't ring him when that's on telly!

Aly can be contacted through his website and blog:

www.darkrising.co.uk
www.alyfell.blogspot.co.uk

Dark Rising - The Art of Aly Fell

Book design by Grassy Knoll Studios.

Published by SQP Inc.
PO Box 248 - Columbus NJ 08022

Sal Quartuccio & Bob Keenan - Publishers

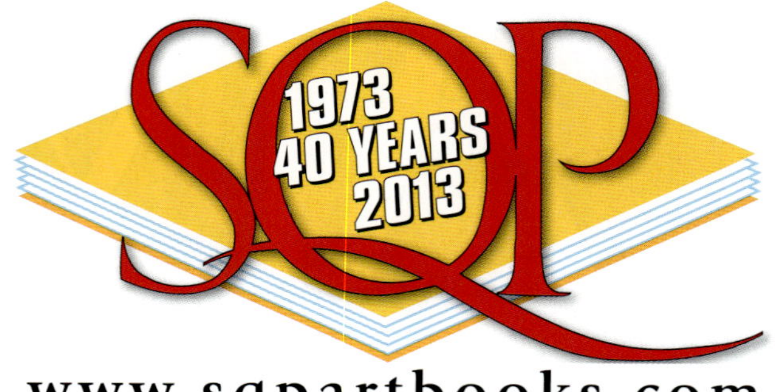

PIXIE
LIQUID
TEA
SUGAR
I ♥ KY
Shopping
Kitty Litter
Cream
Ball of String!
KiTTY
AF'05

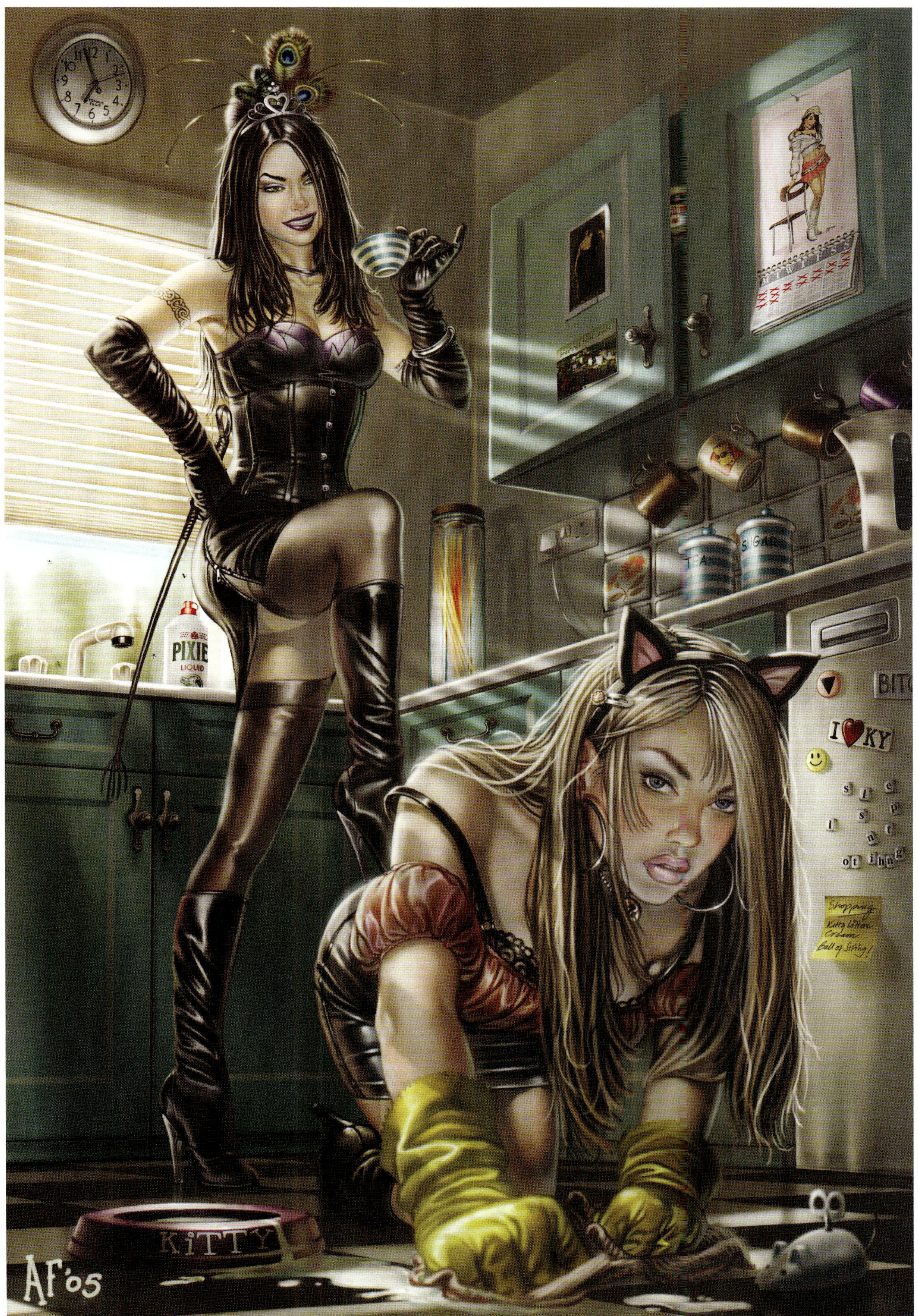

Bad Kitty

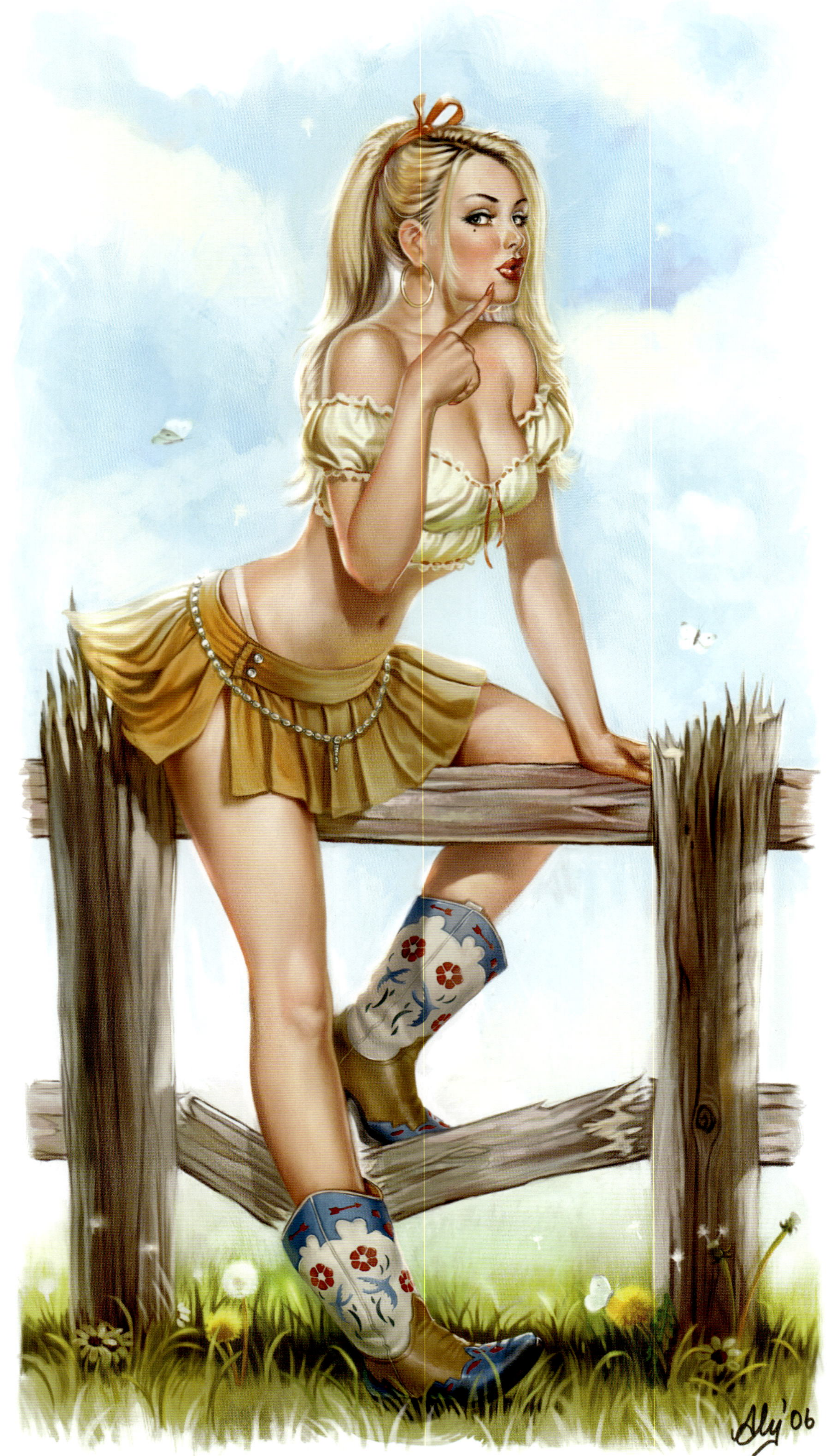

Ooops!

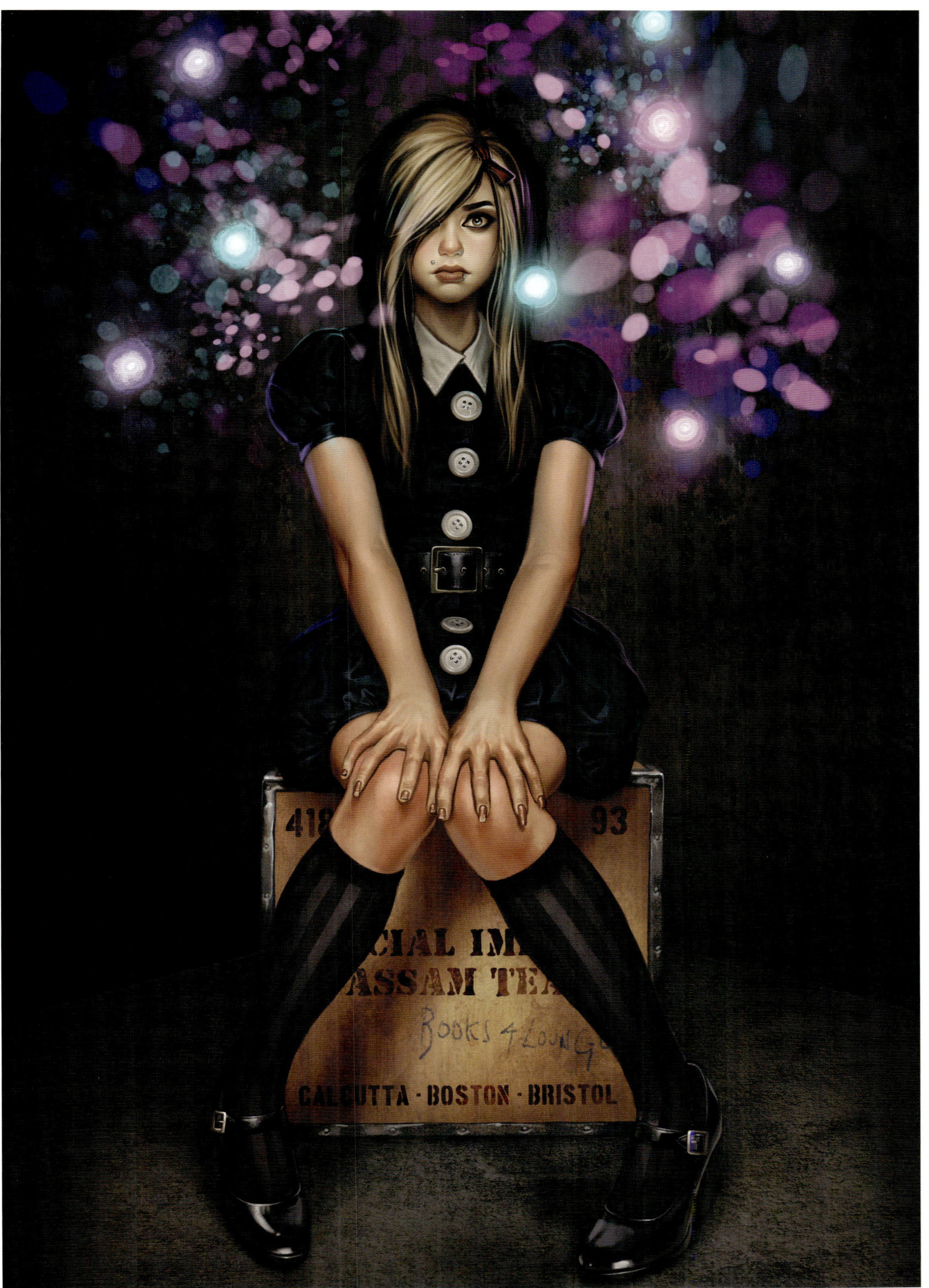

Sophie Sees - after John Wright

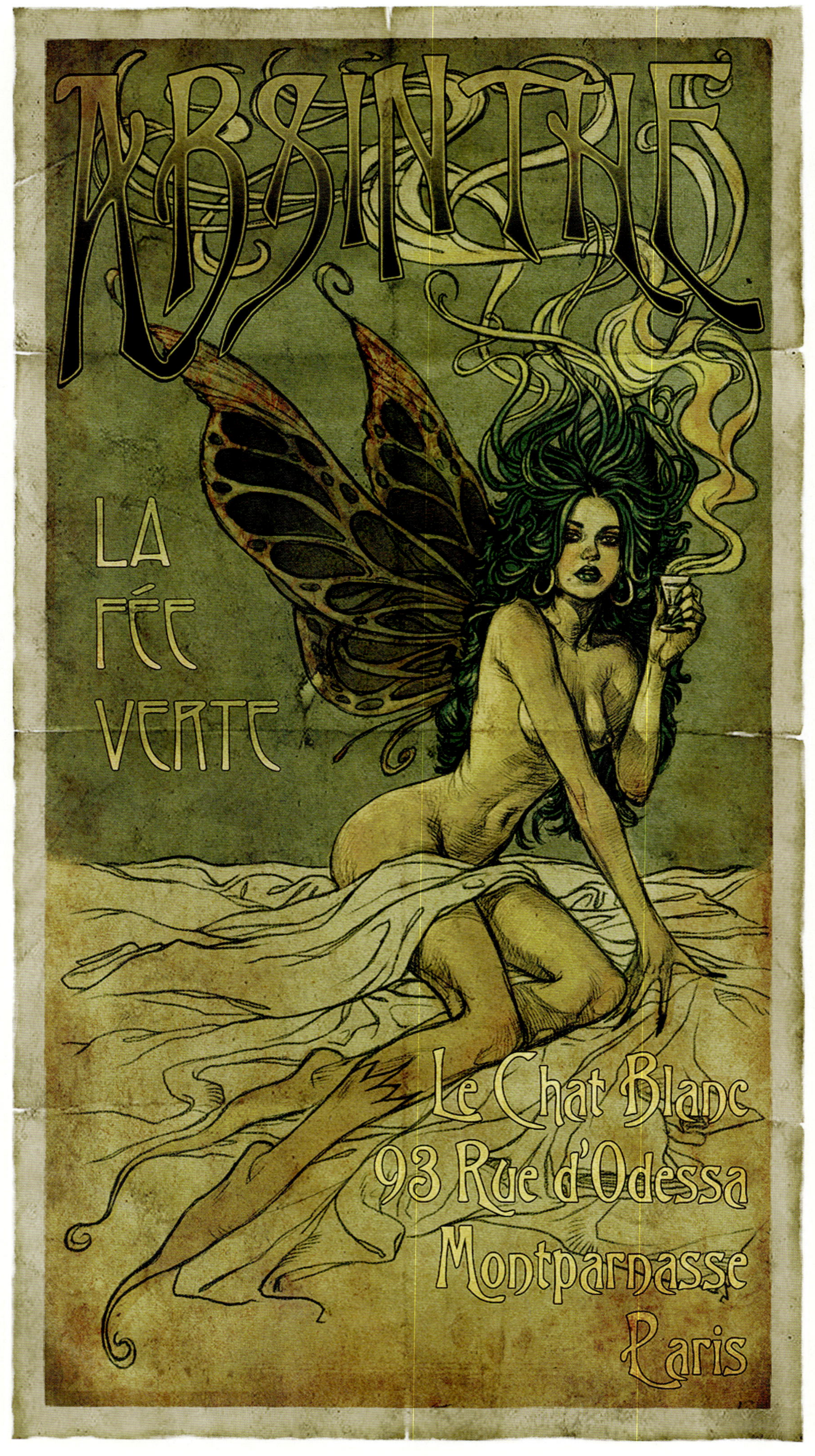

Absinthe Fairy

VOLTS
Scotch
ACID
GRIFFIN
Invisible Hold!
To Mary luv Frank
abby Normal
HAIR SPRAY
GRIFFIN
HAIR
SPRAY
HAIR SPRAY
Aly '07

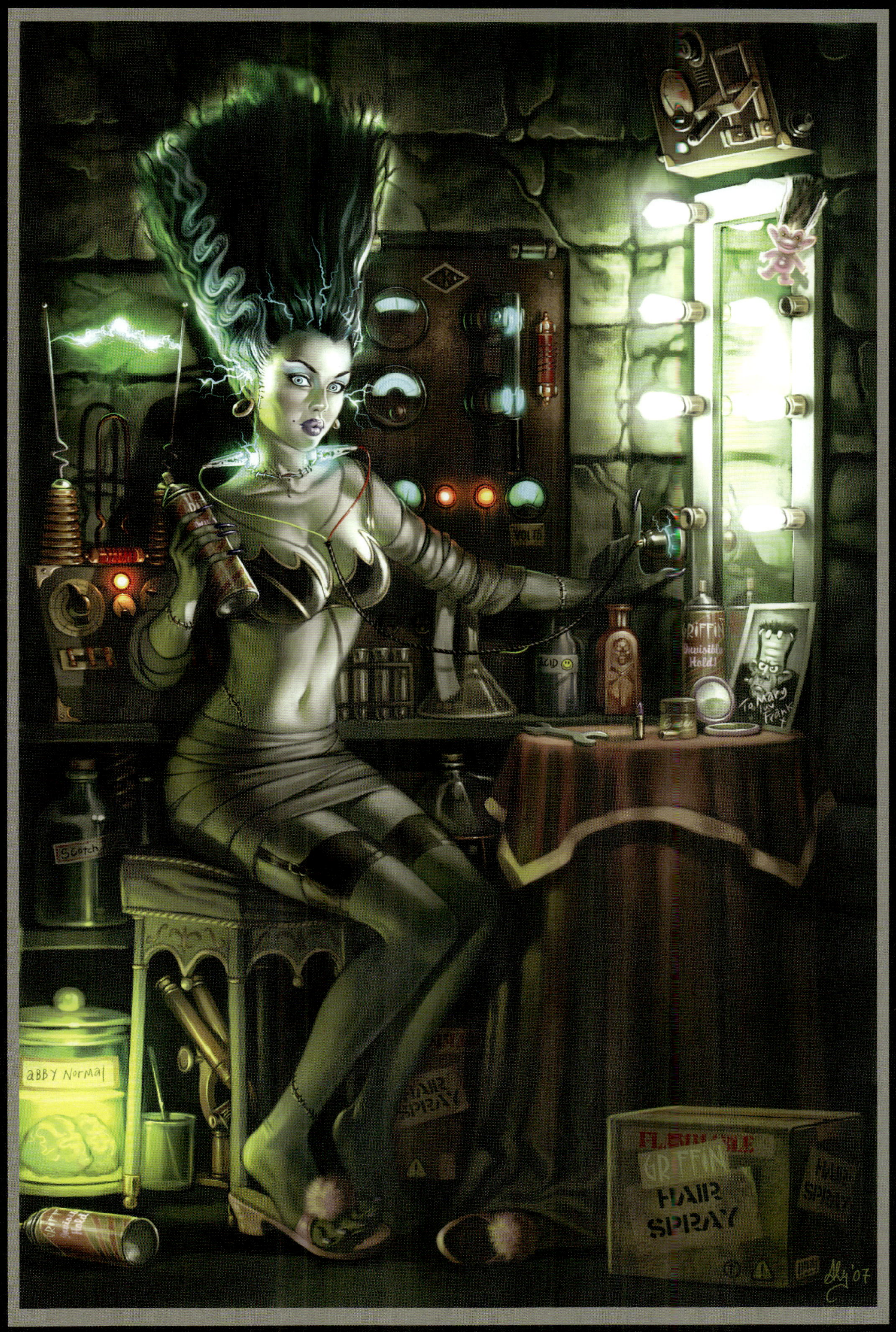

Charge!

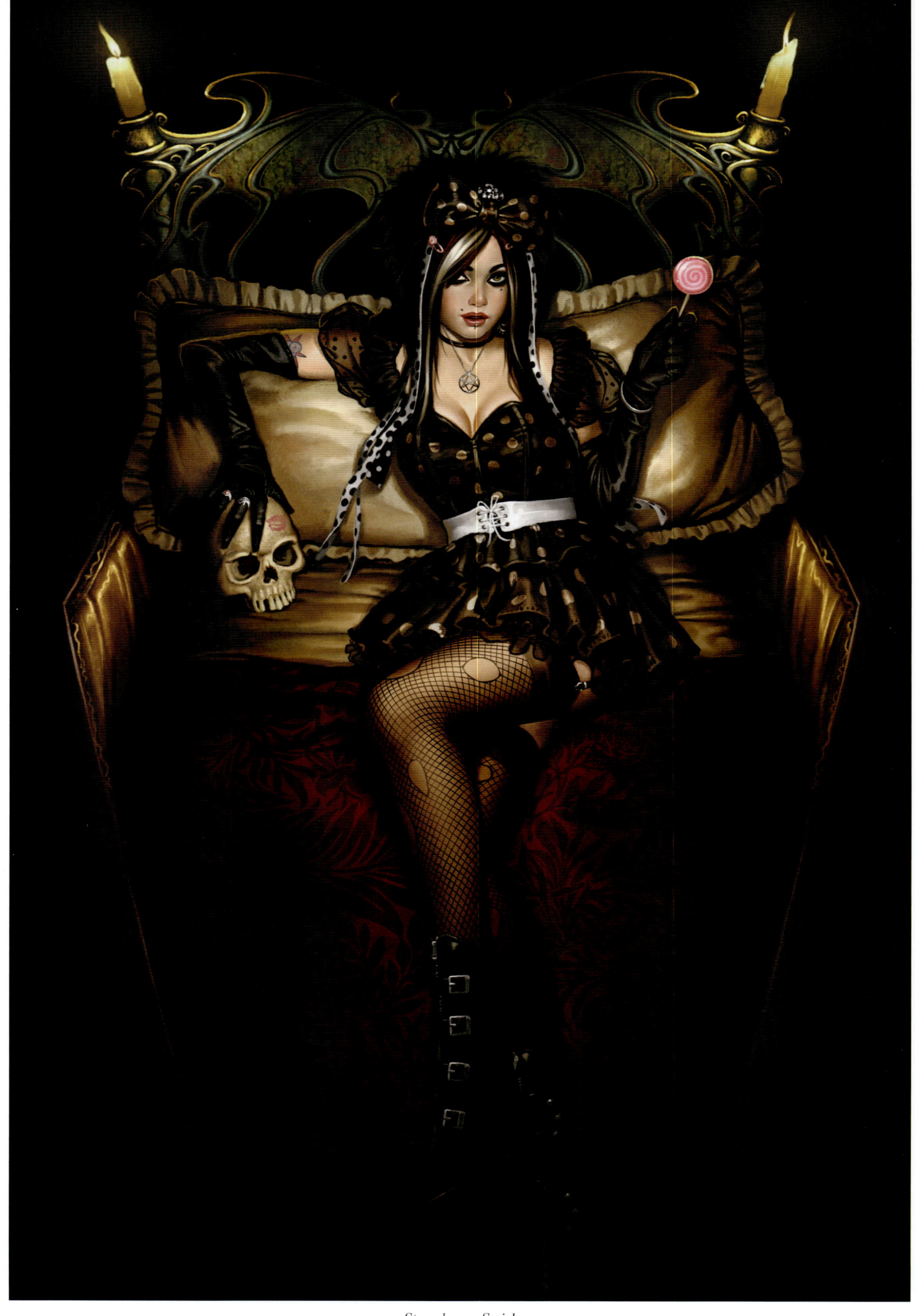

Strawberry Swirl

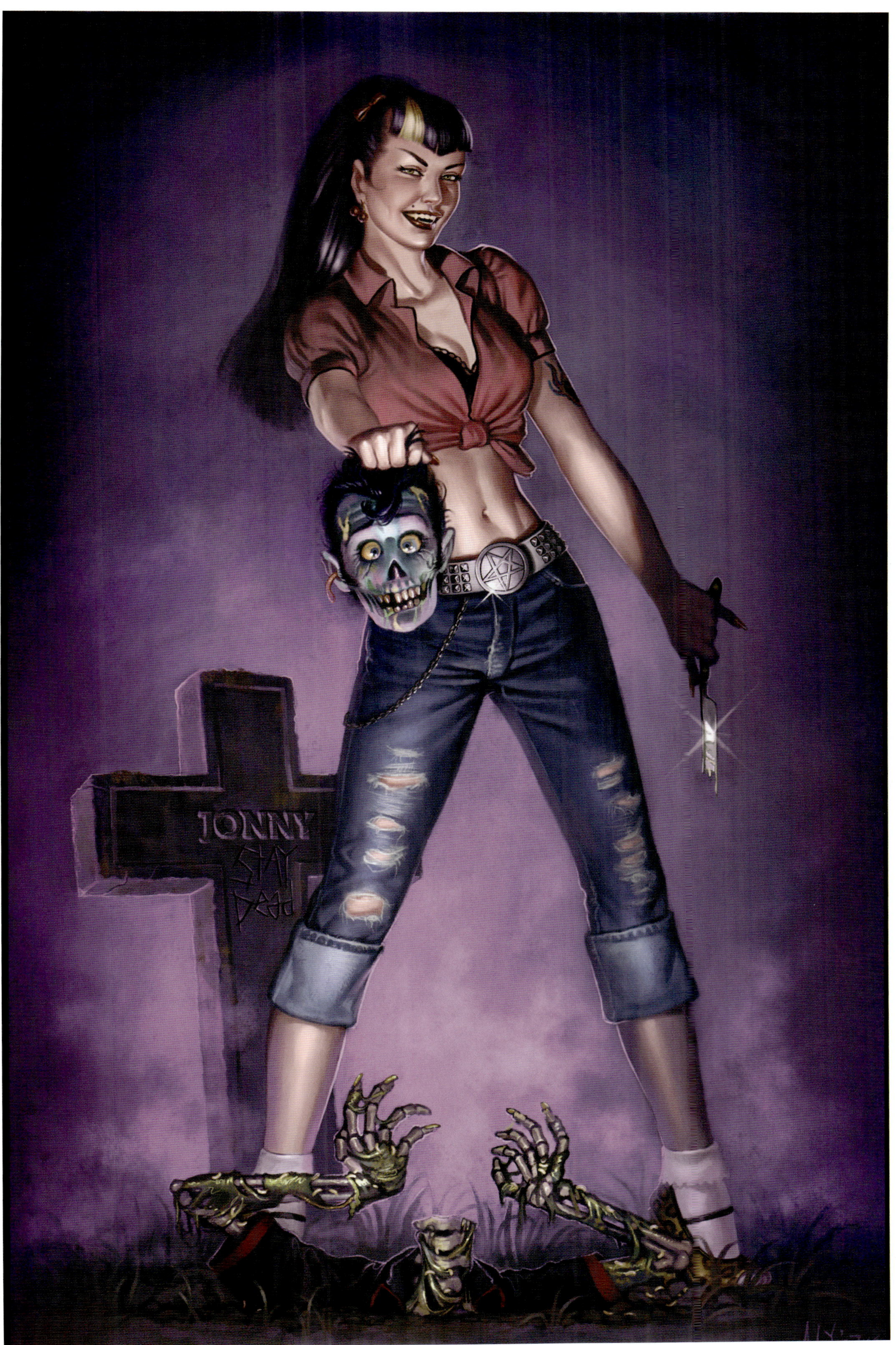

Johnny Stay Dead

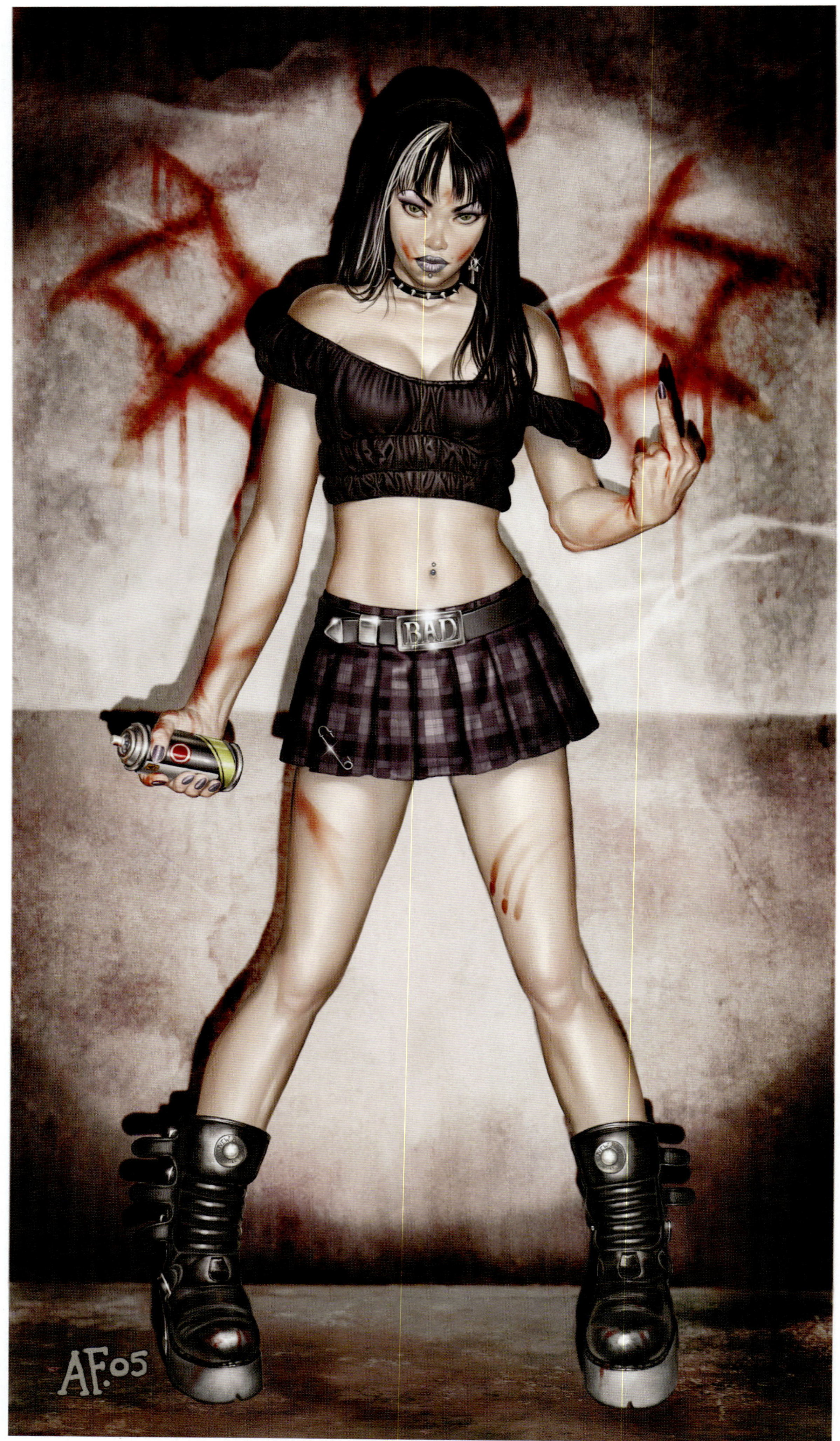

Li'l Devil

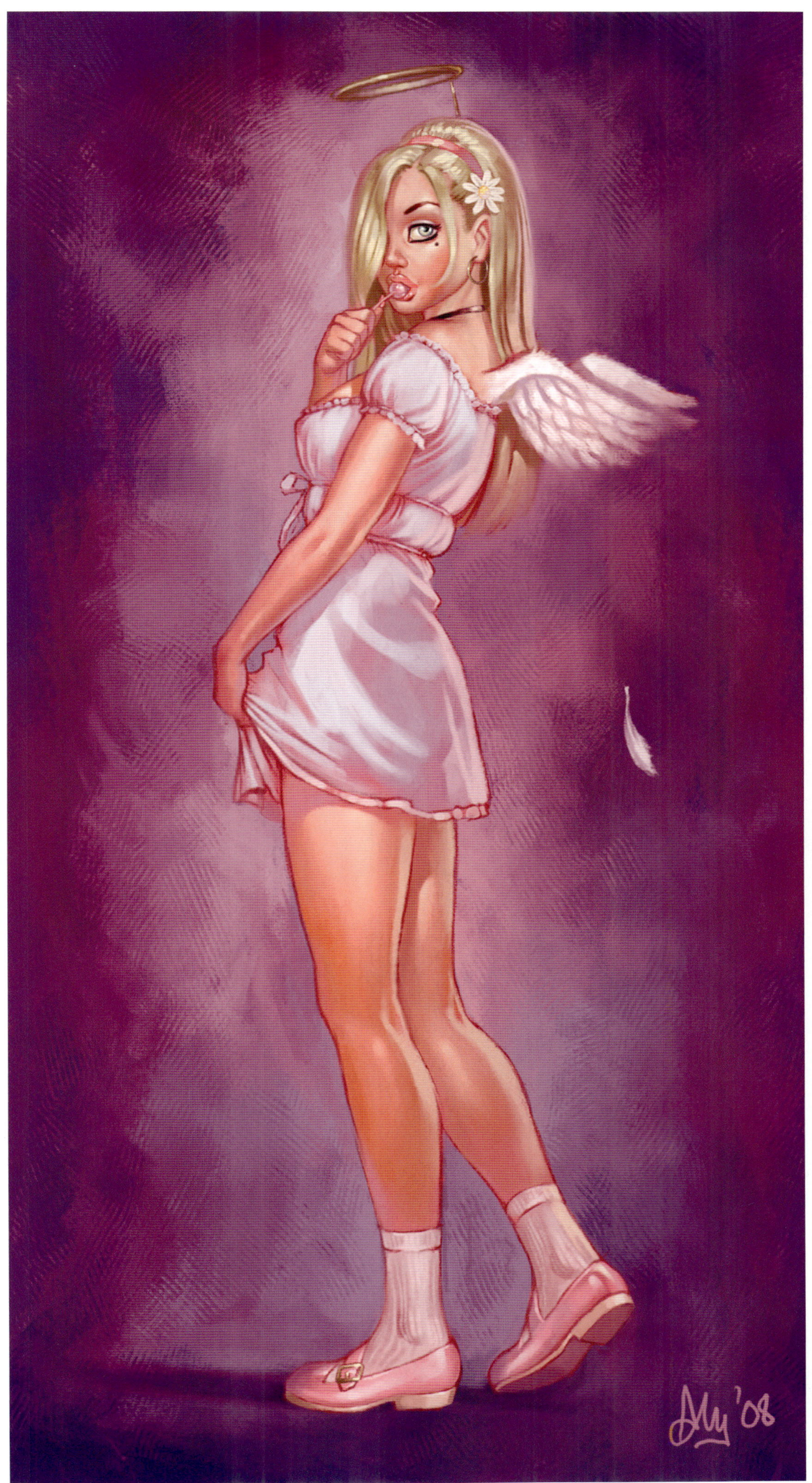

Fall From Grace

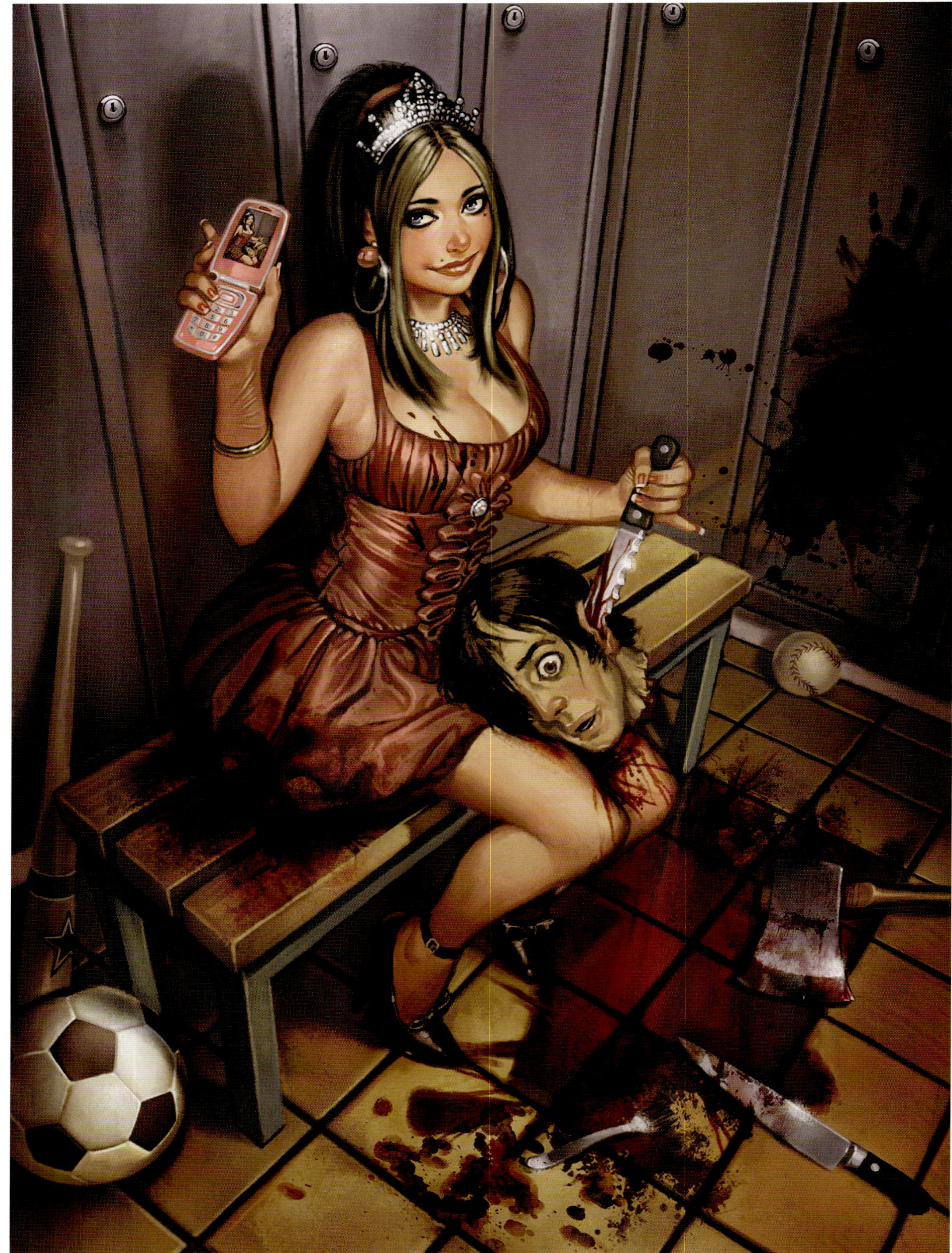

Tiffany May

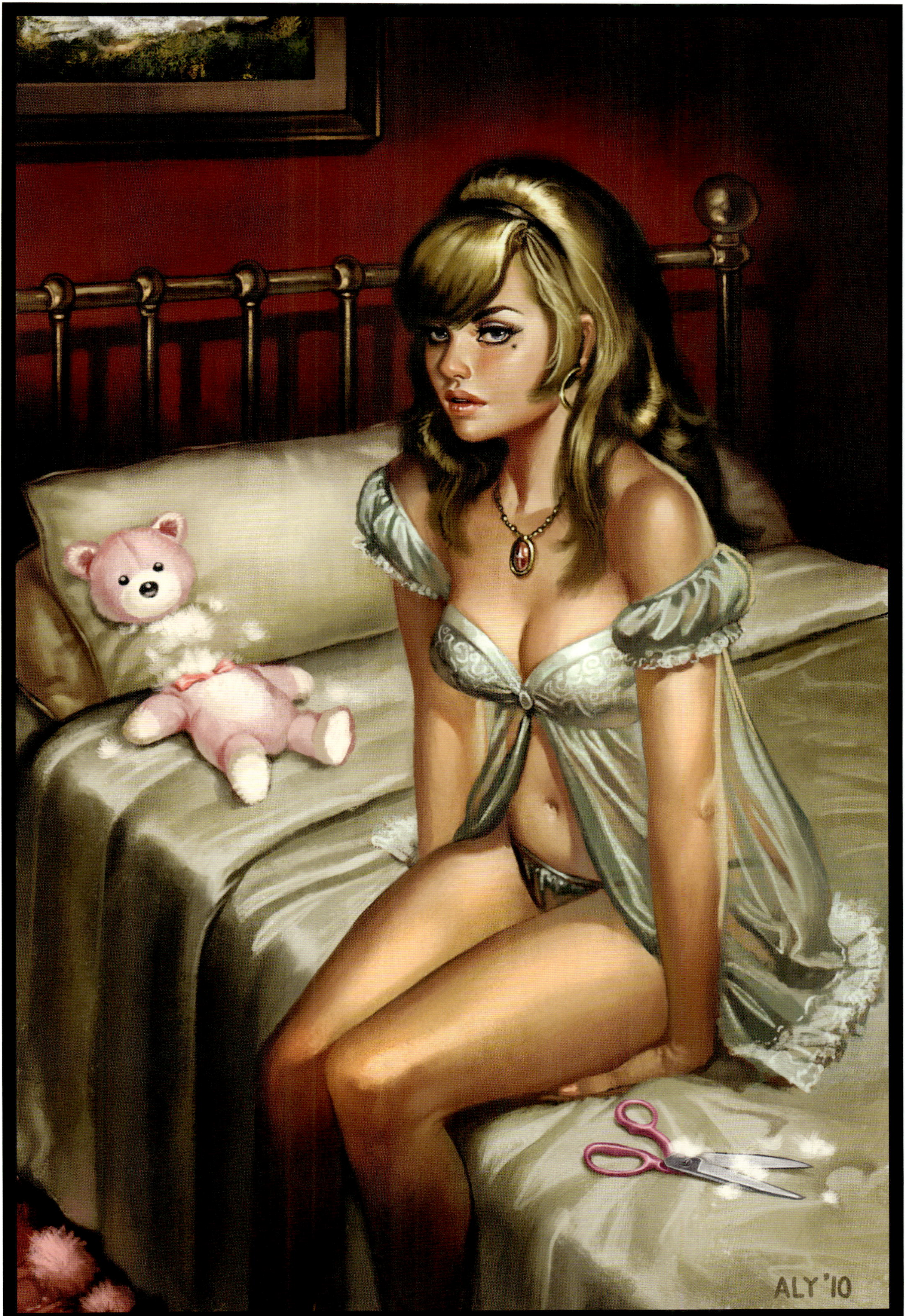

Bad Bear Day

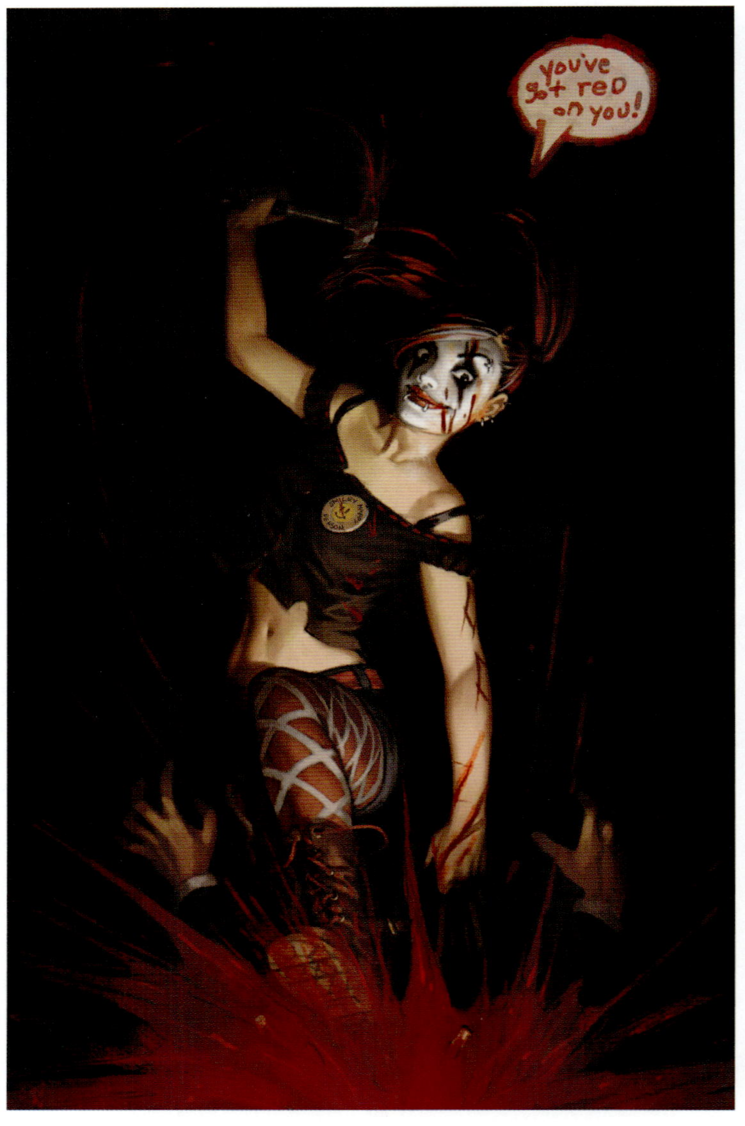

Harley

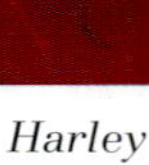

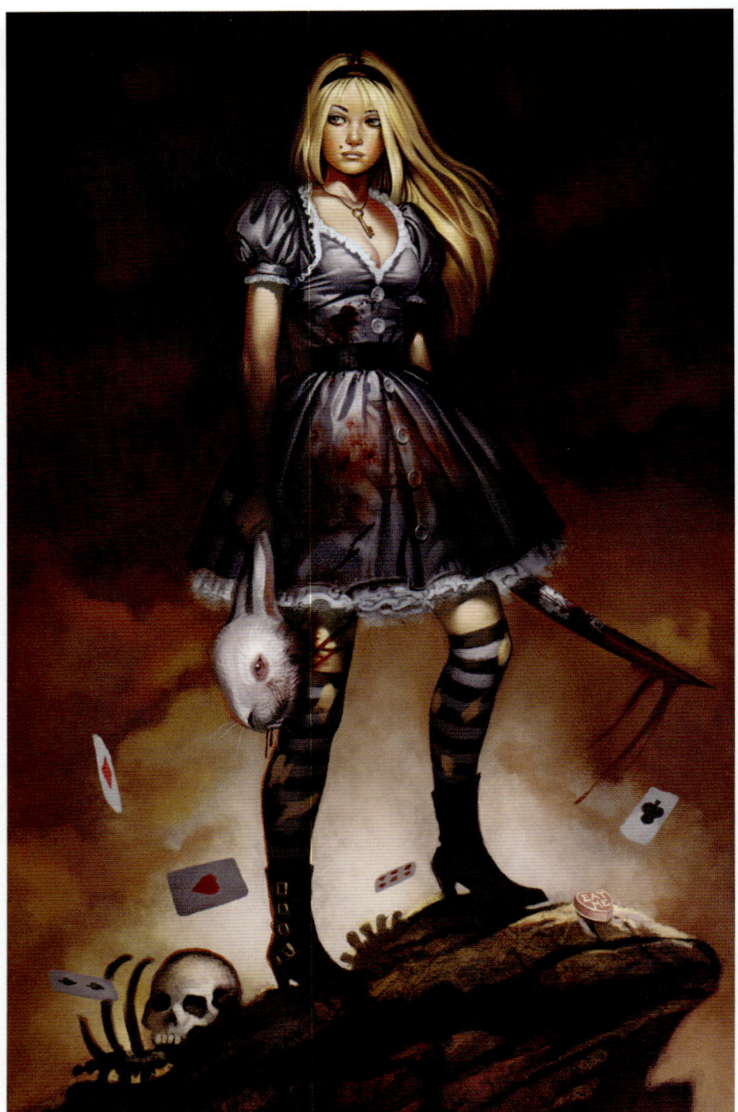

Warrior Alice

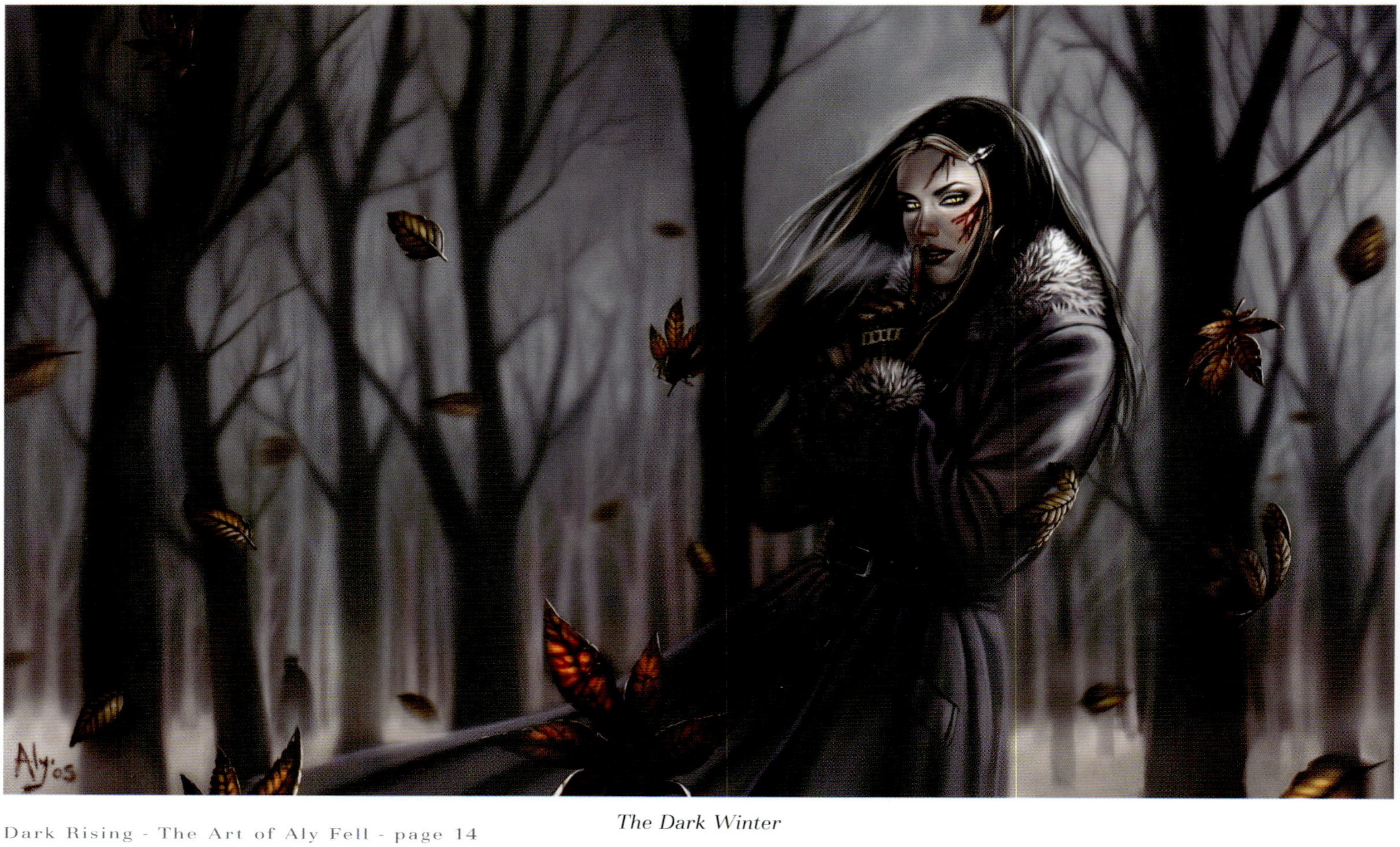

The Dark Winter

Monday to Friday
5.00pm
Saturday
11.30am
ROSIE POE
POST OFFICE

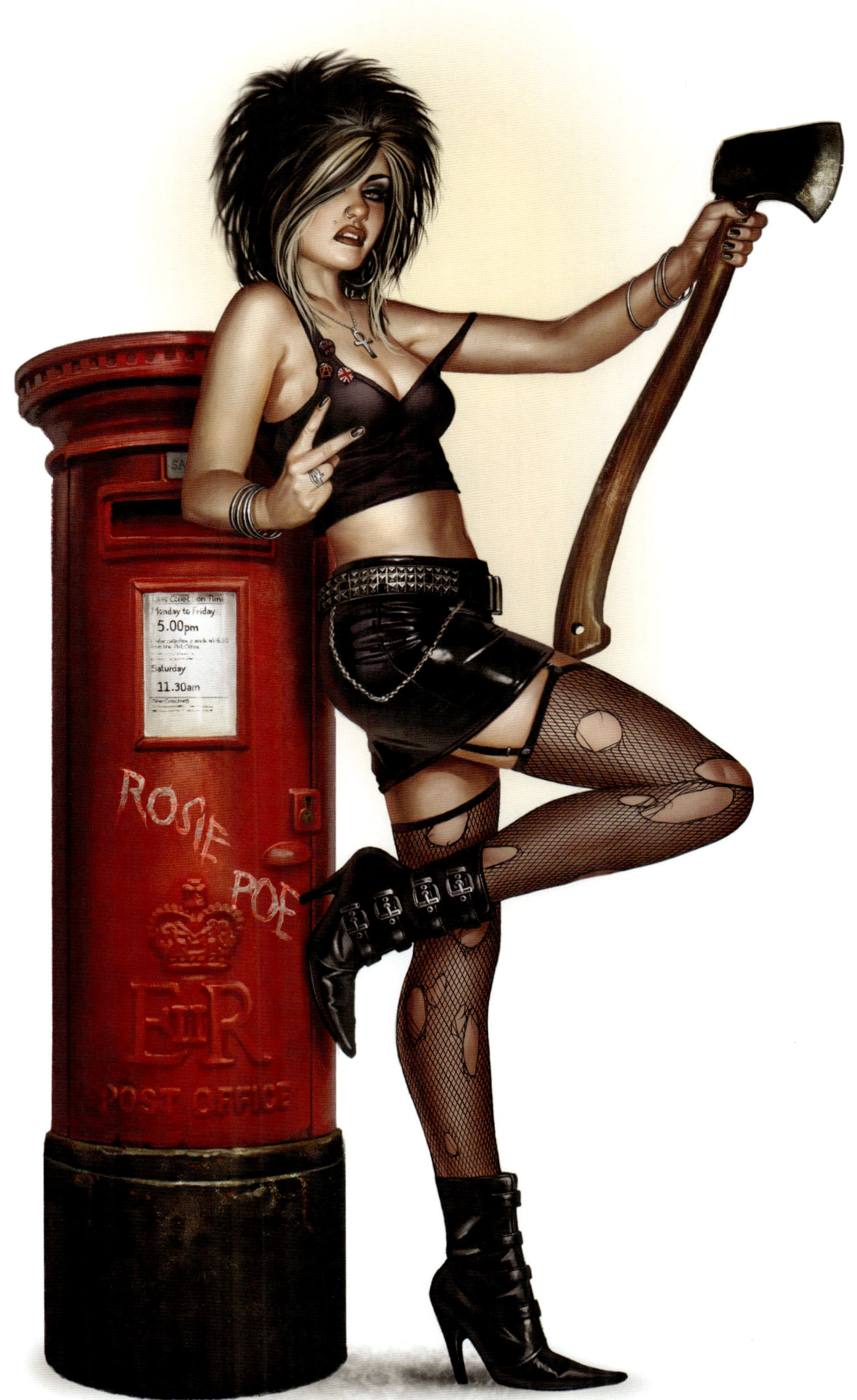

Rosie Poe

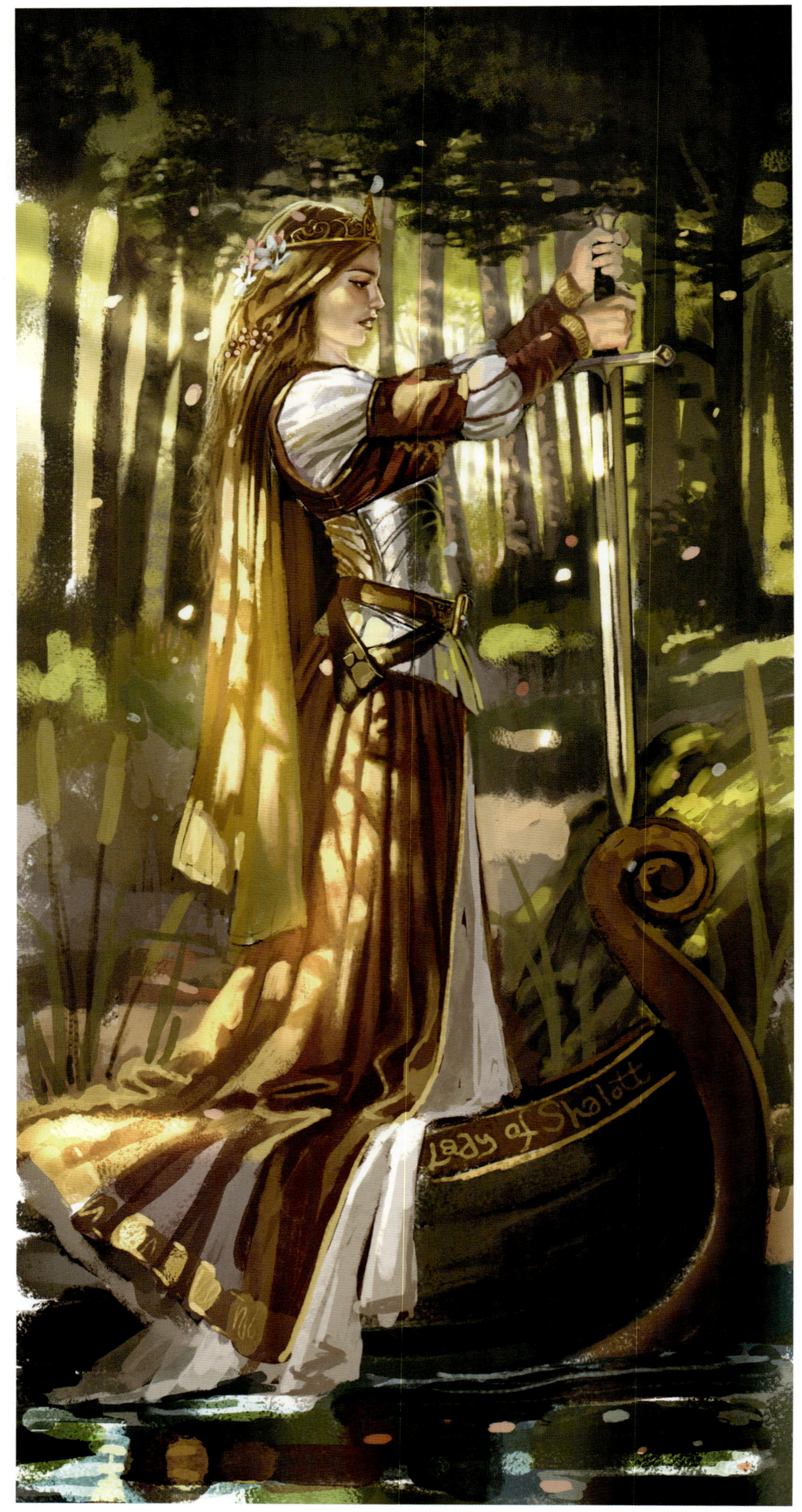

Lady of Shalott

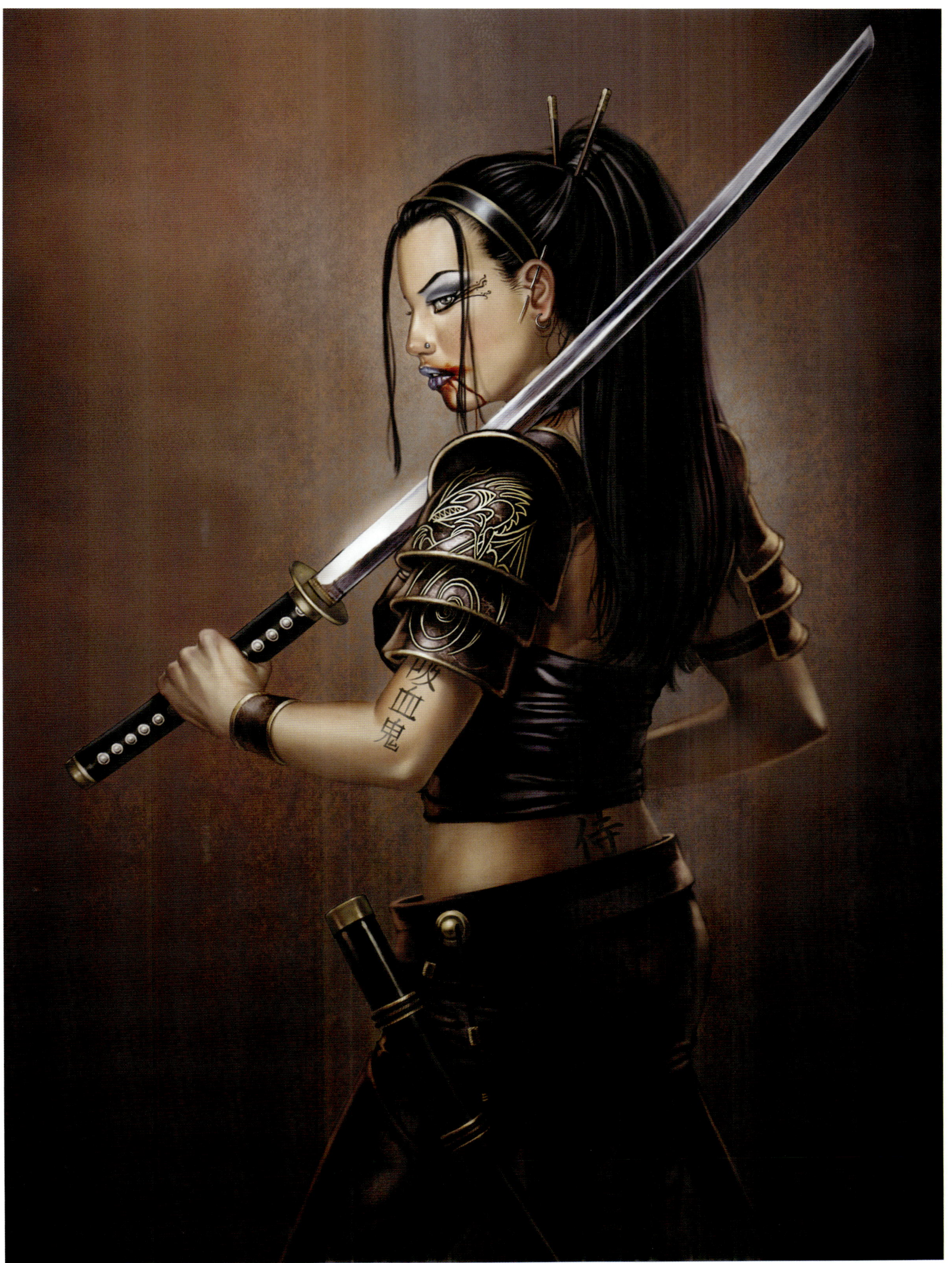

Samurai Vampire

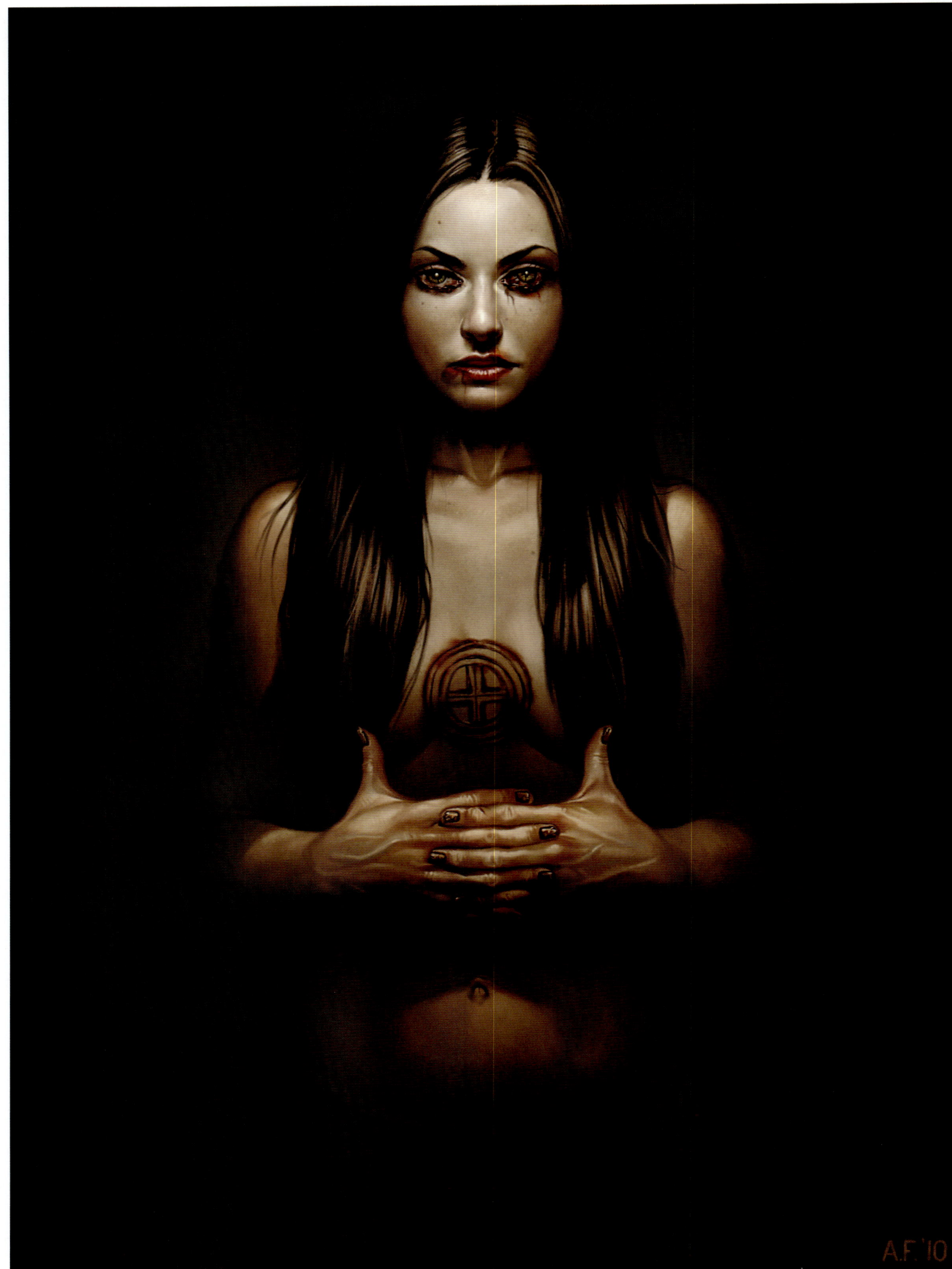

Beast

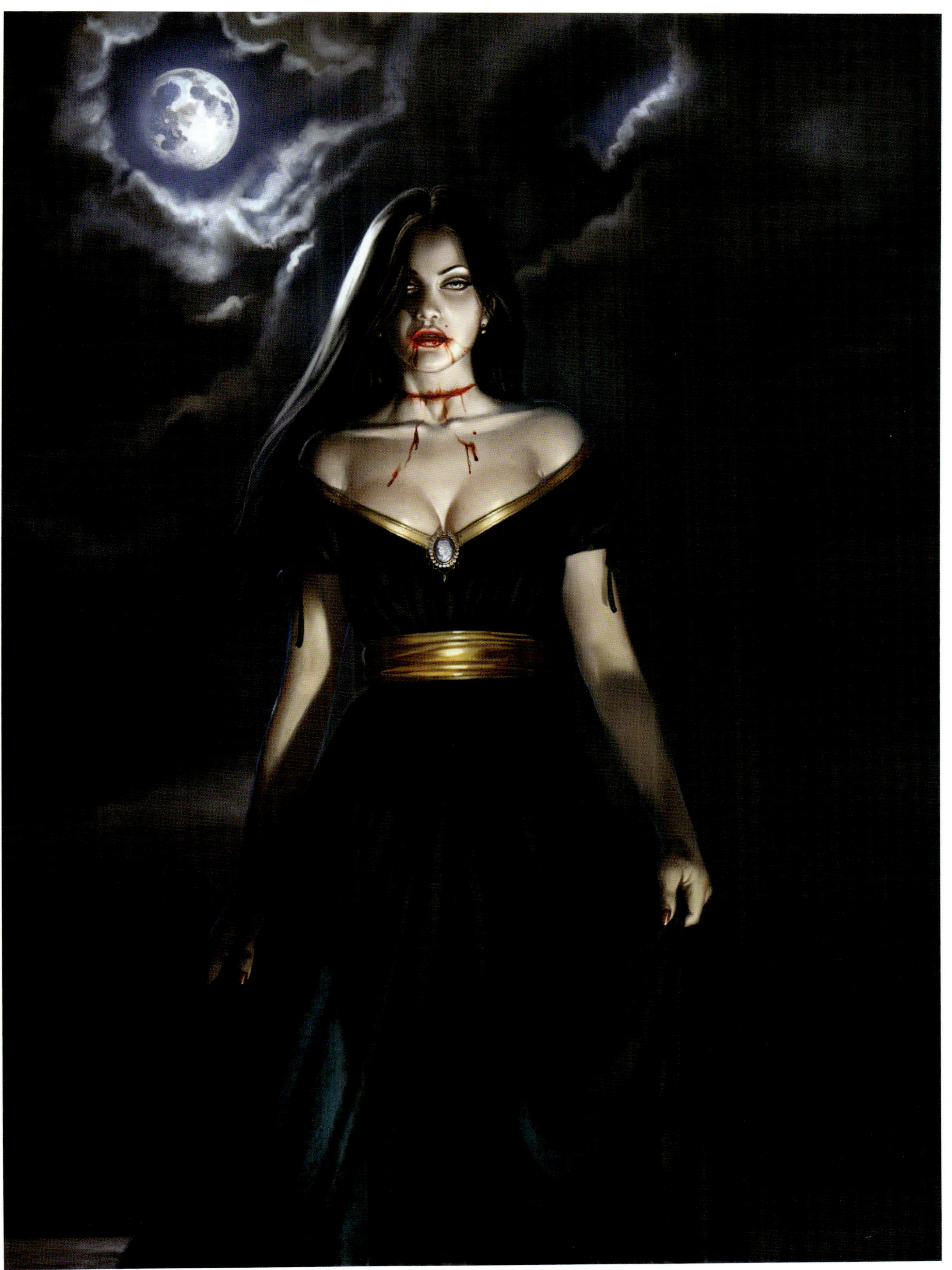

Lucy Harker

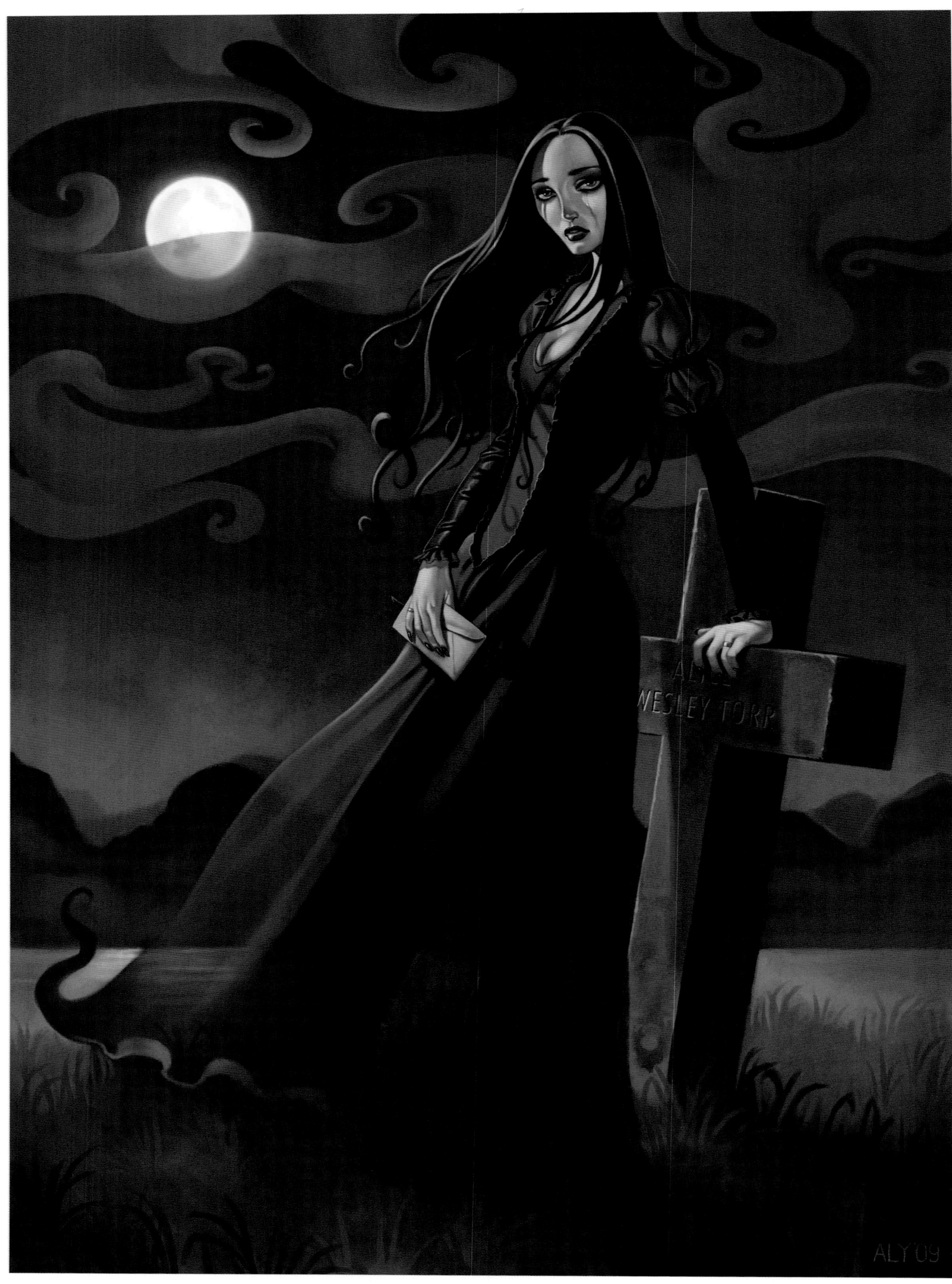

Moonlight You Will Say

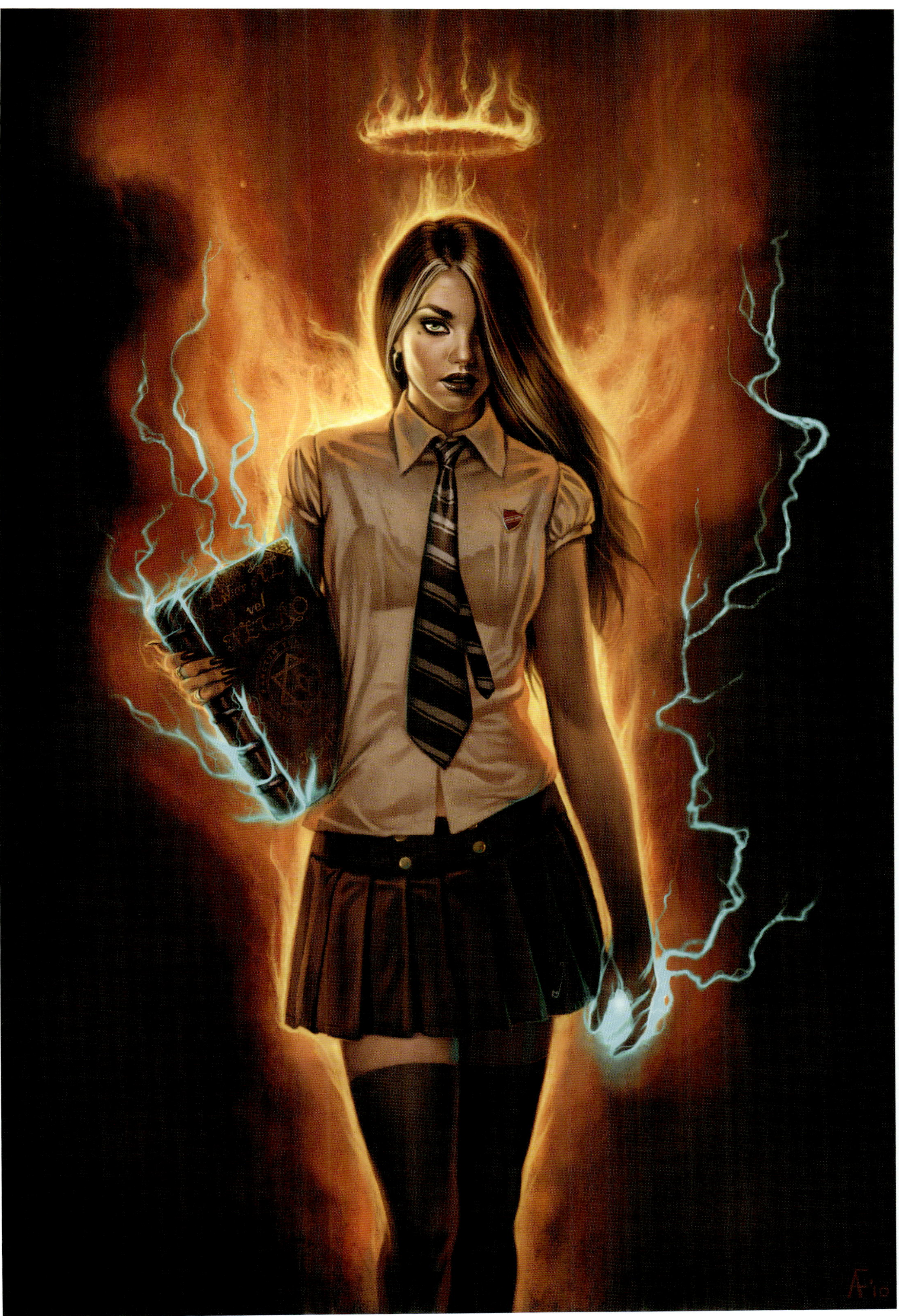

Necromancer

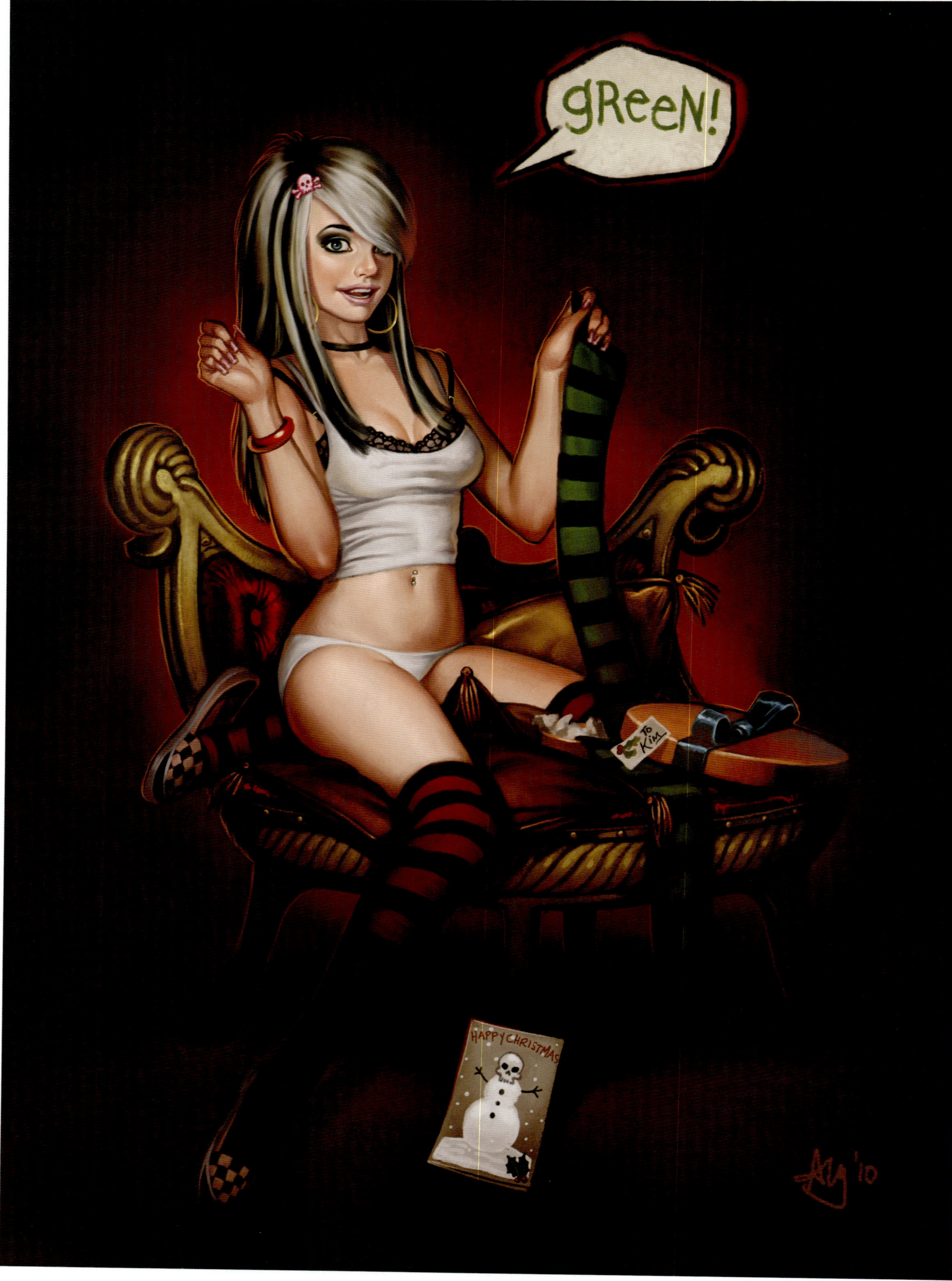

GREEN!

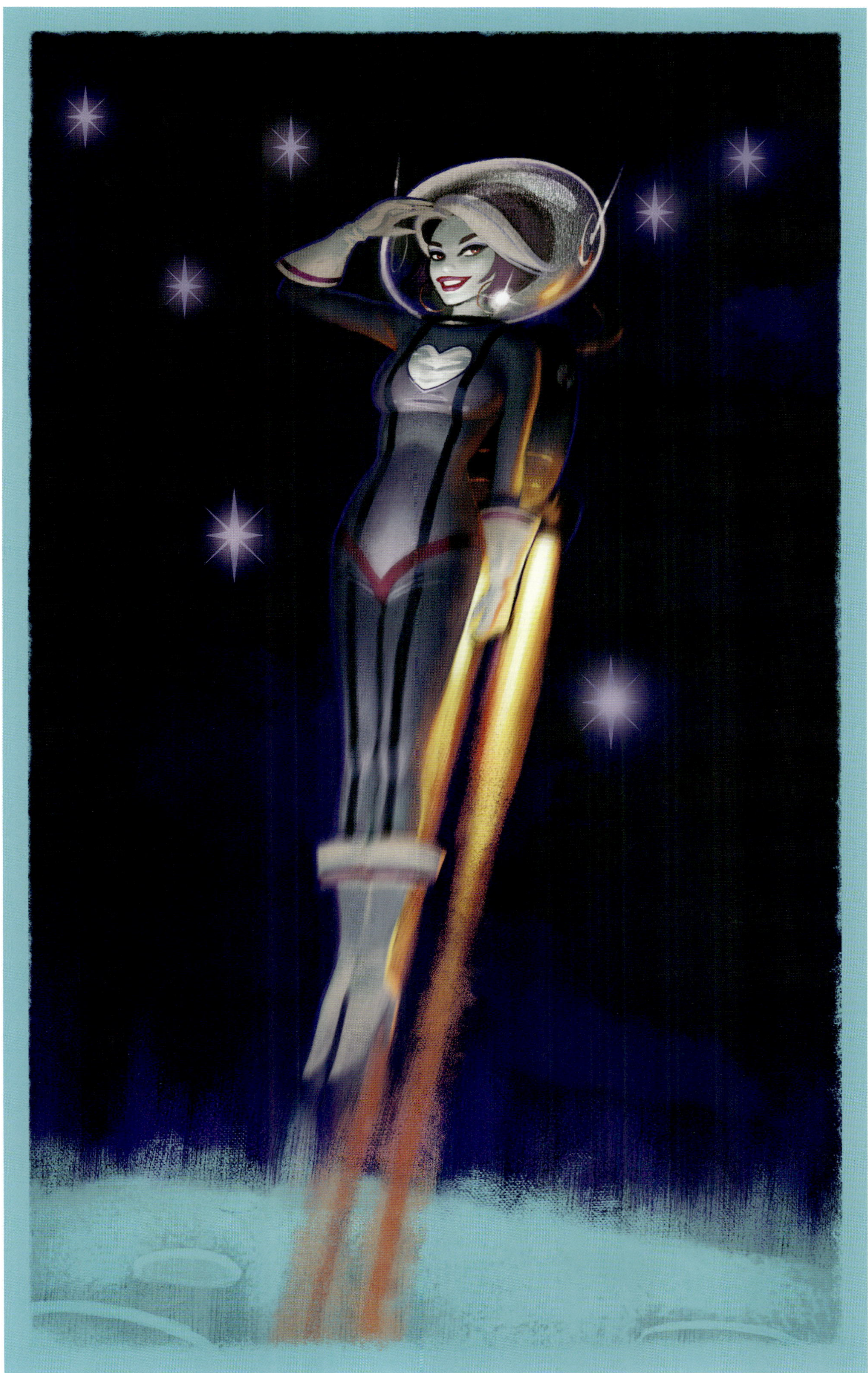

Space Girl

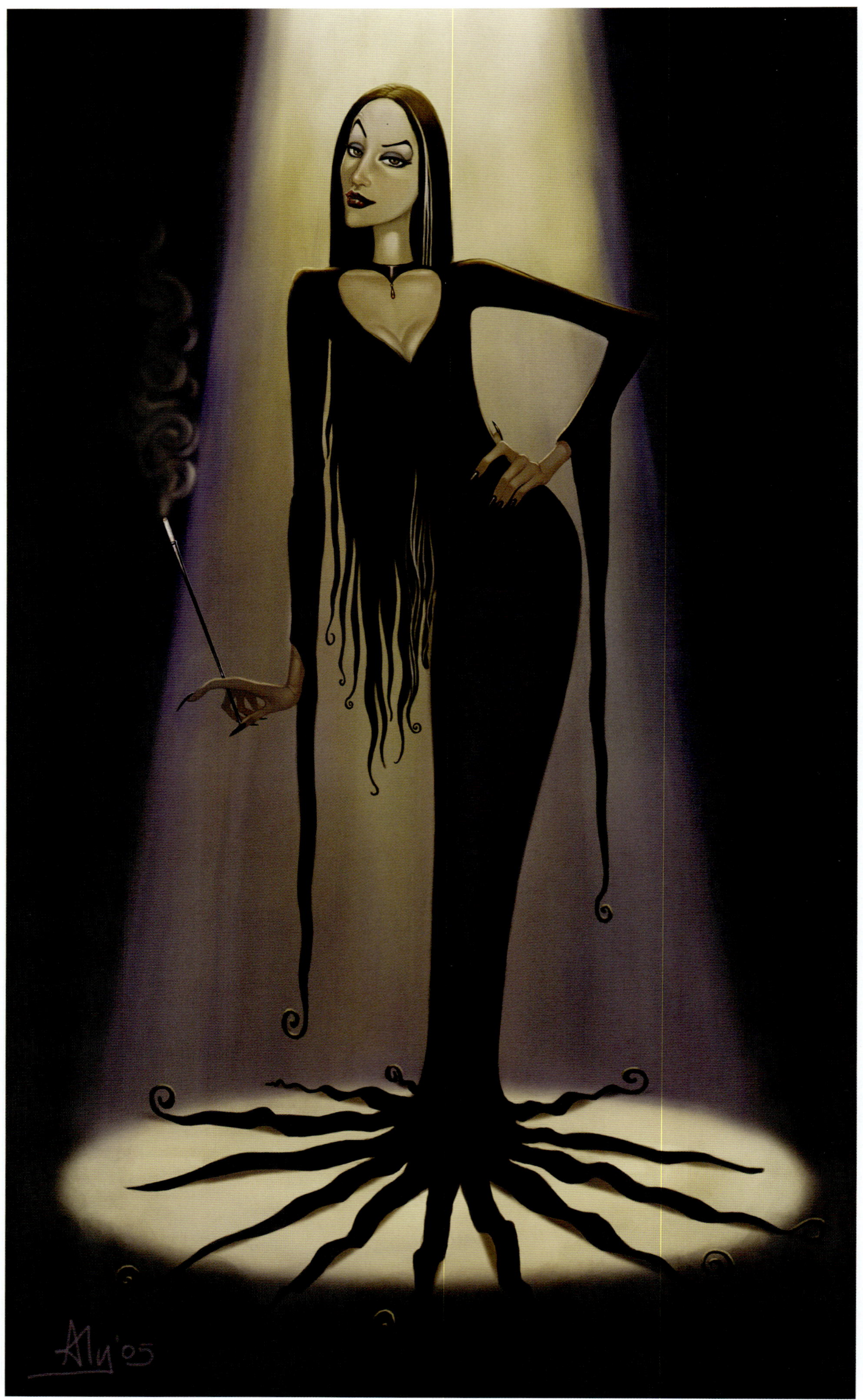

Morticia

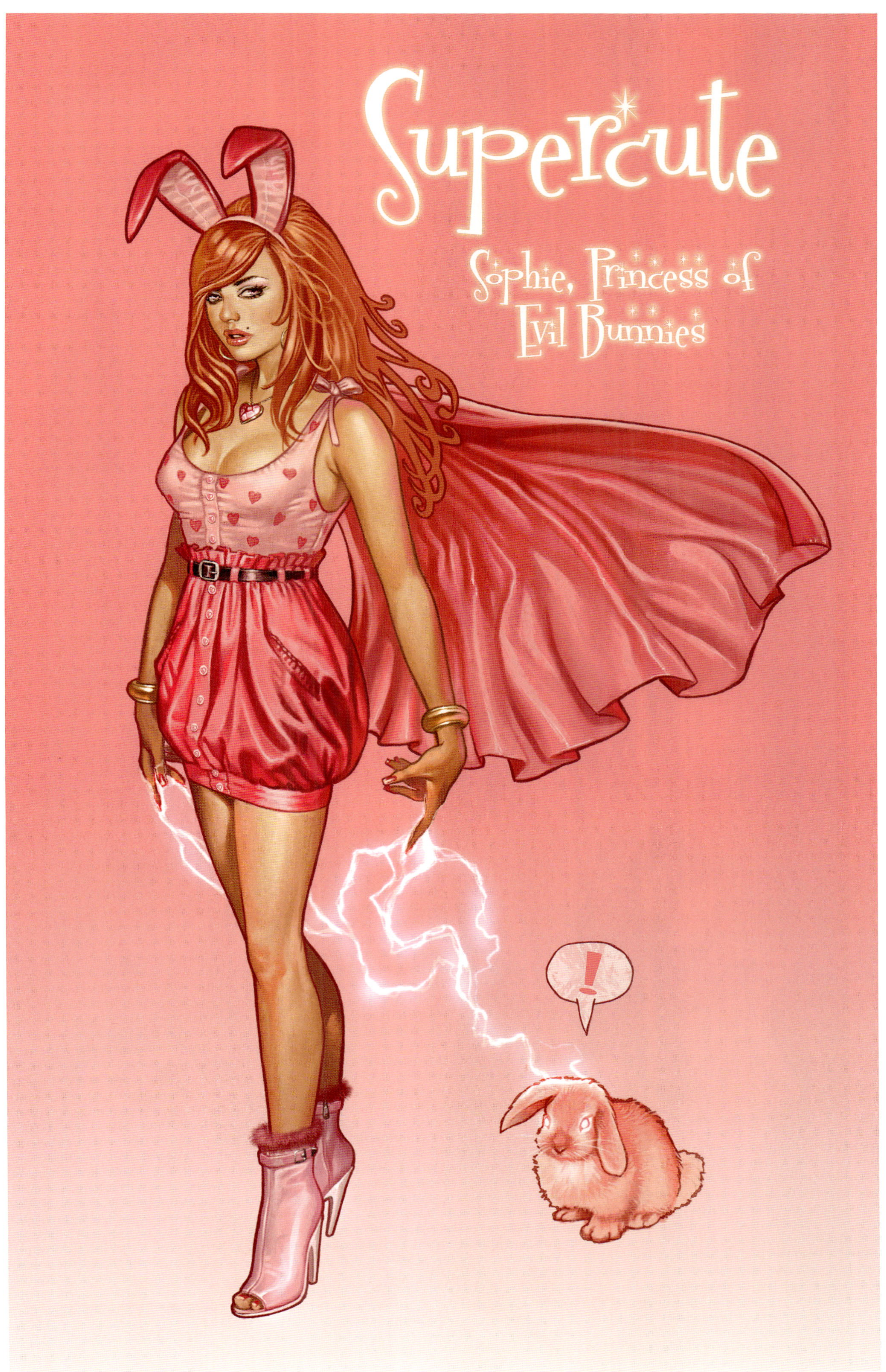

Supercute

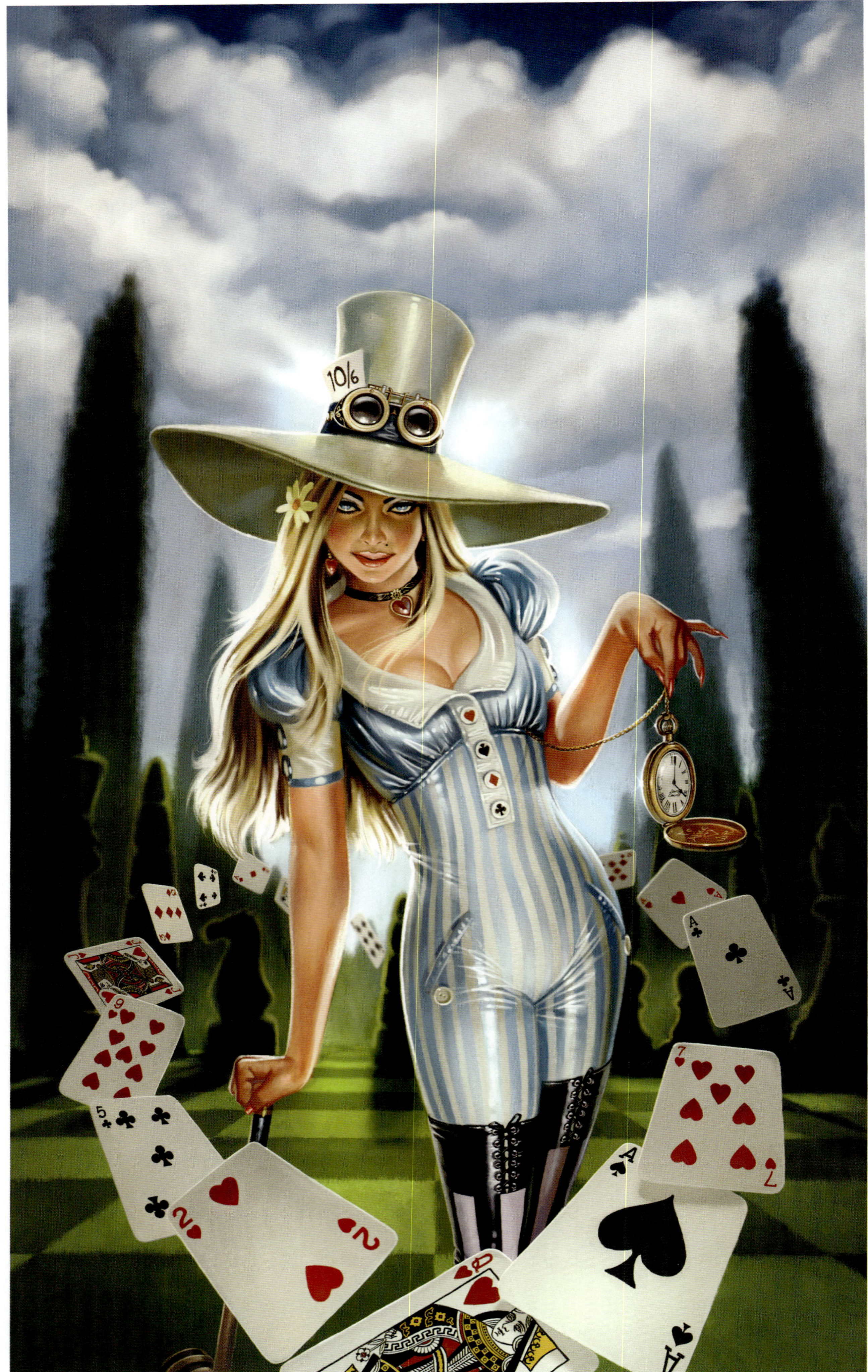

Alice

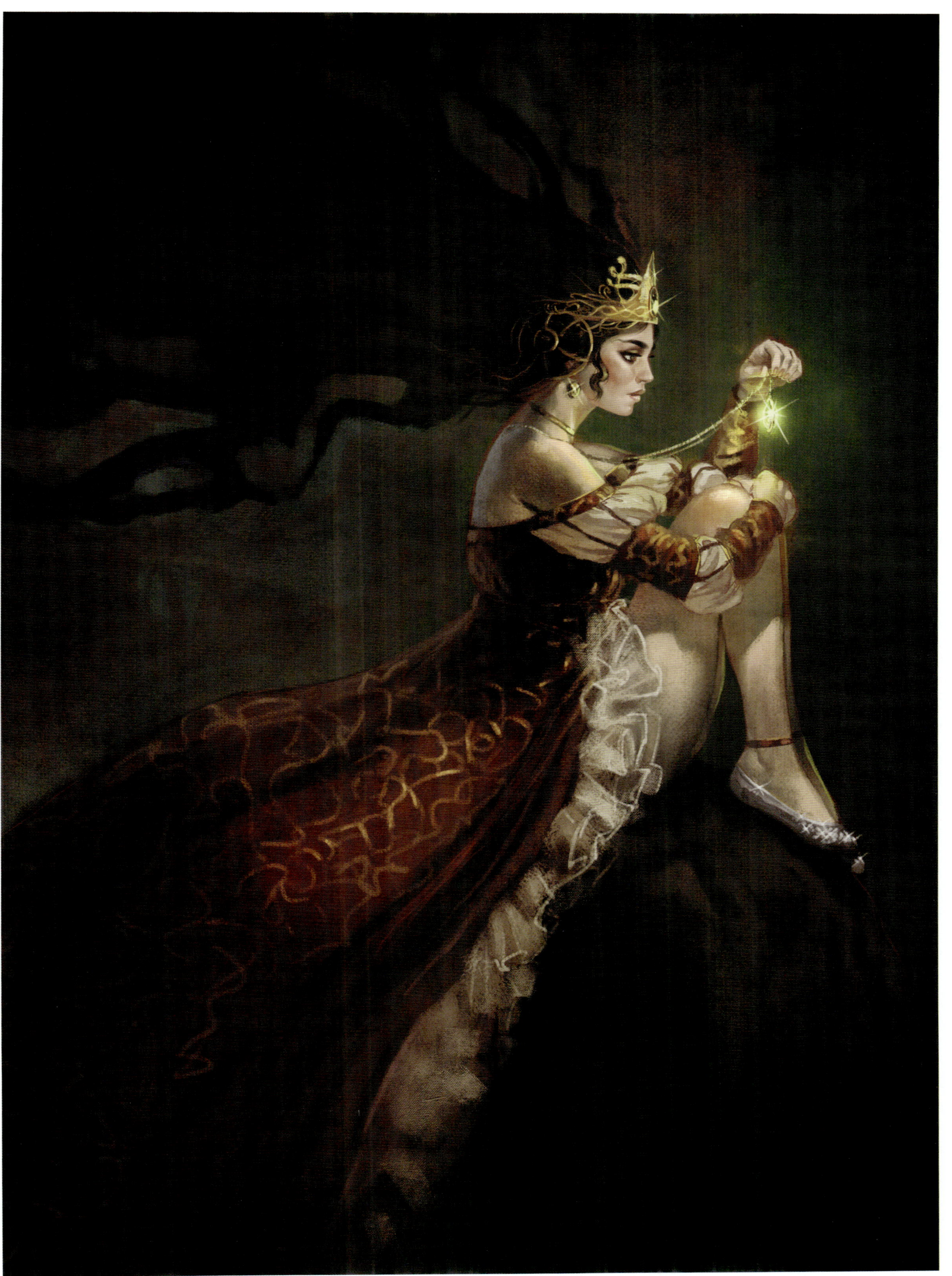

Princess Dorothy

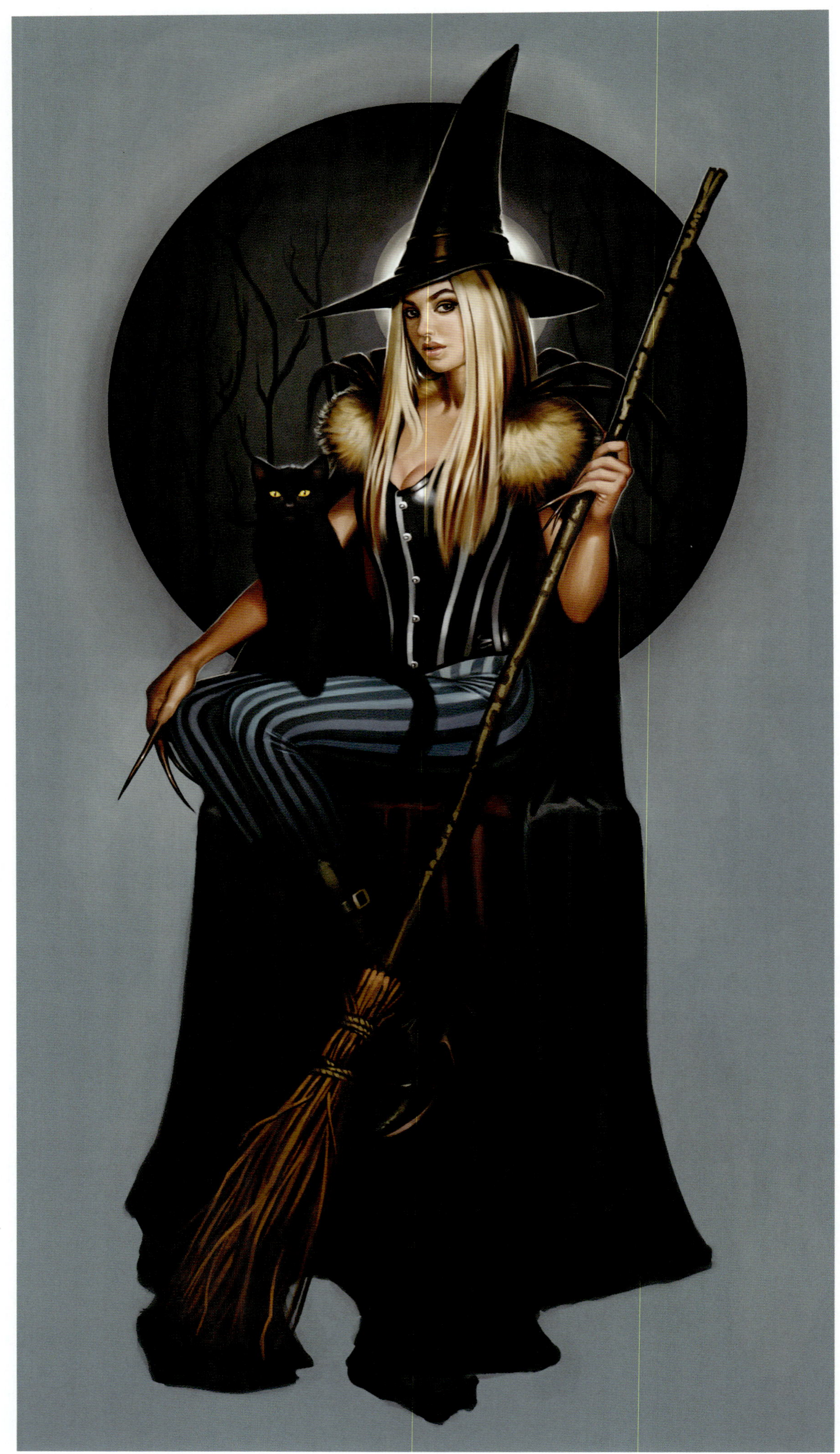

The Winter Witch

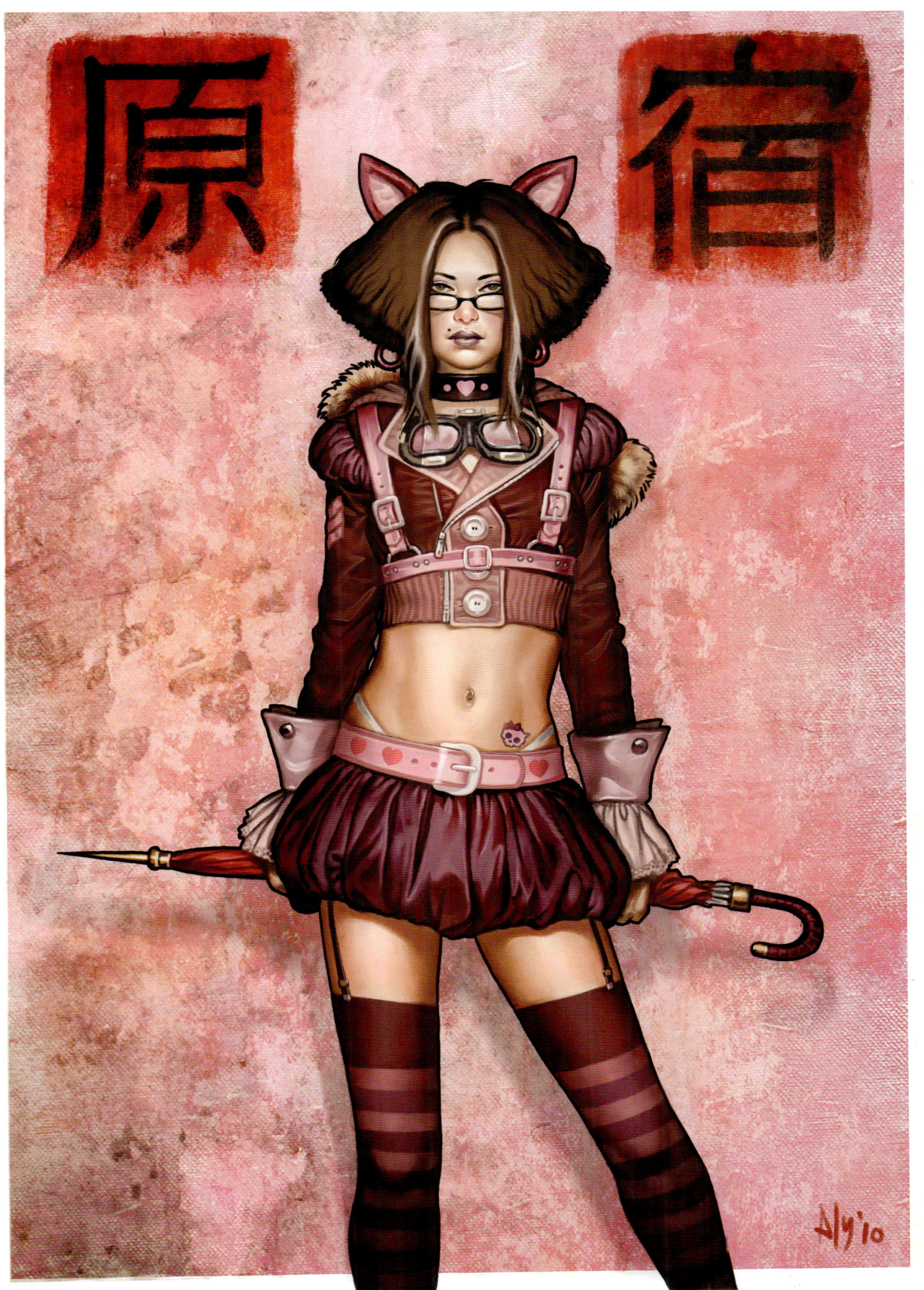

Harajuku

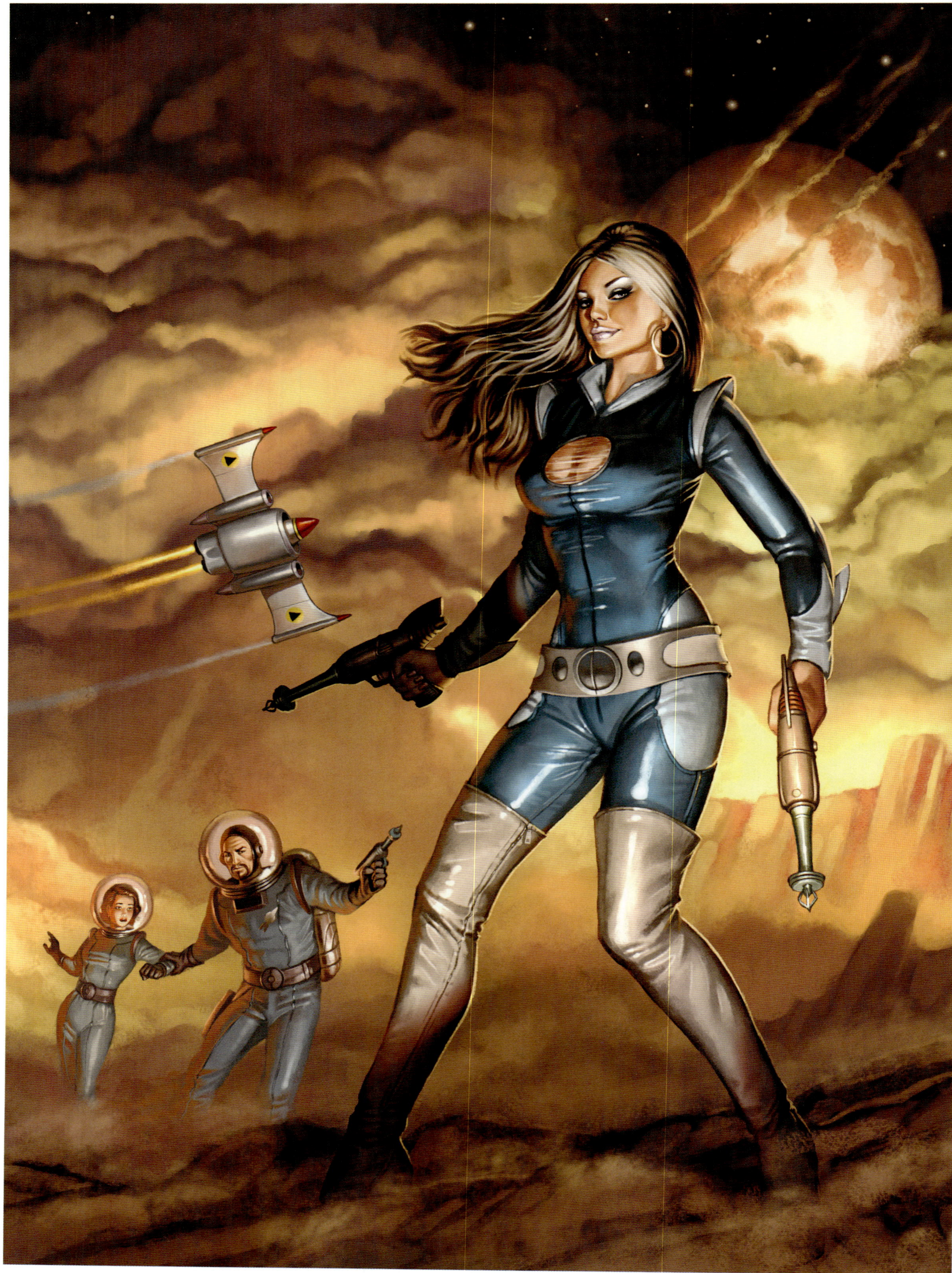

Imagine FX Cover

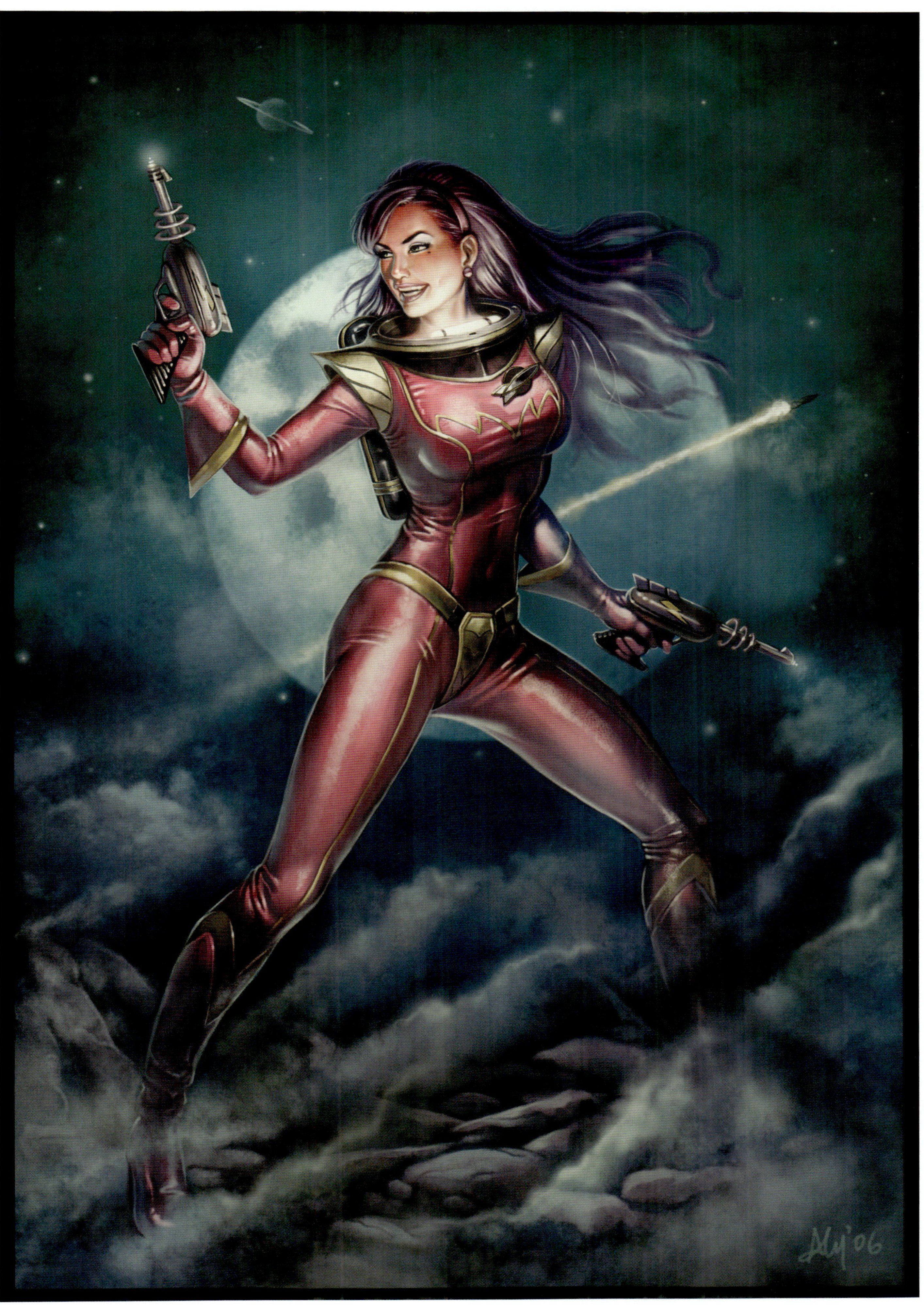

Nancy Goodaim

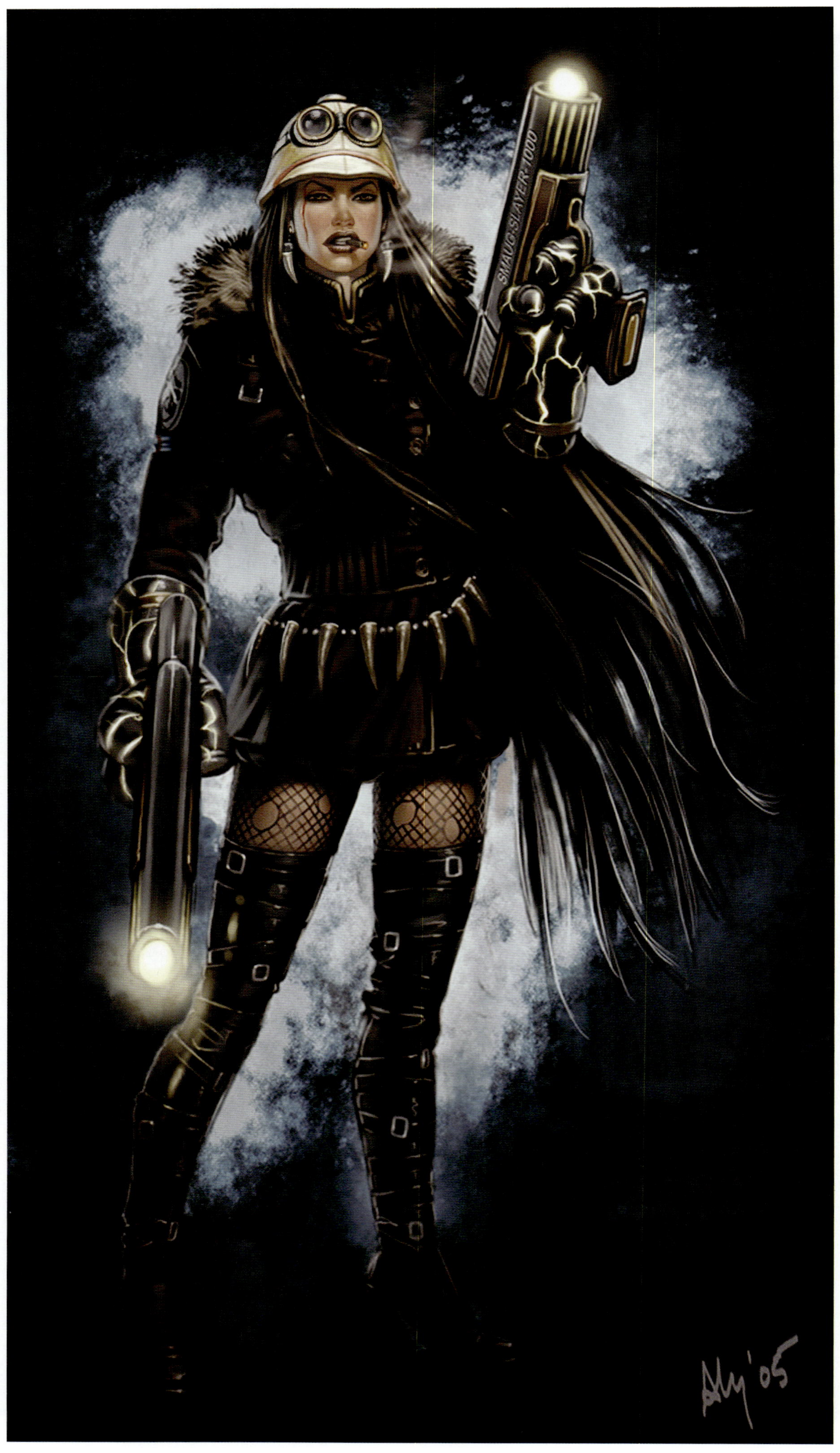

Serran: The Hunter

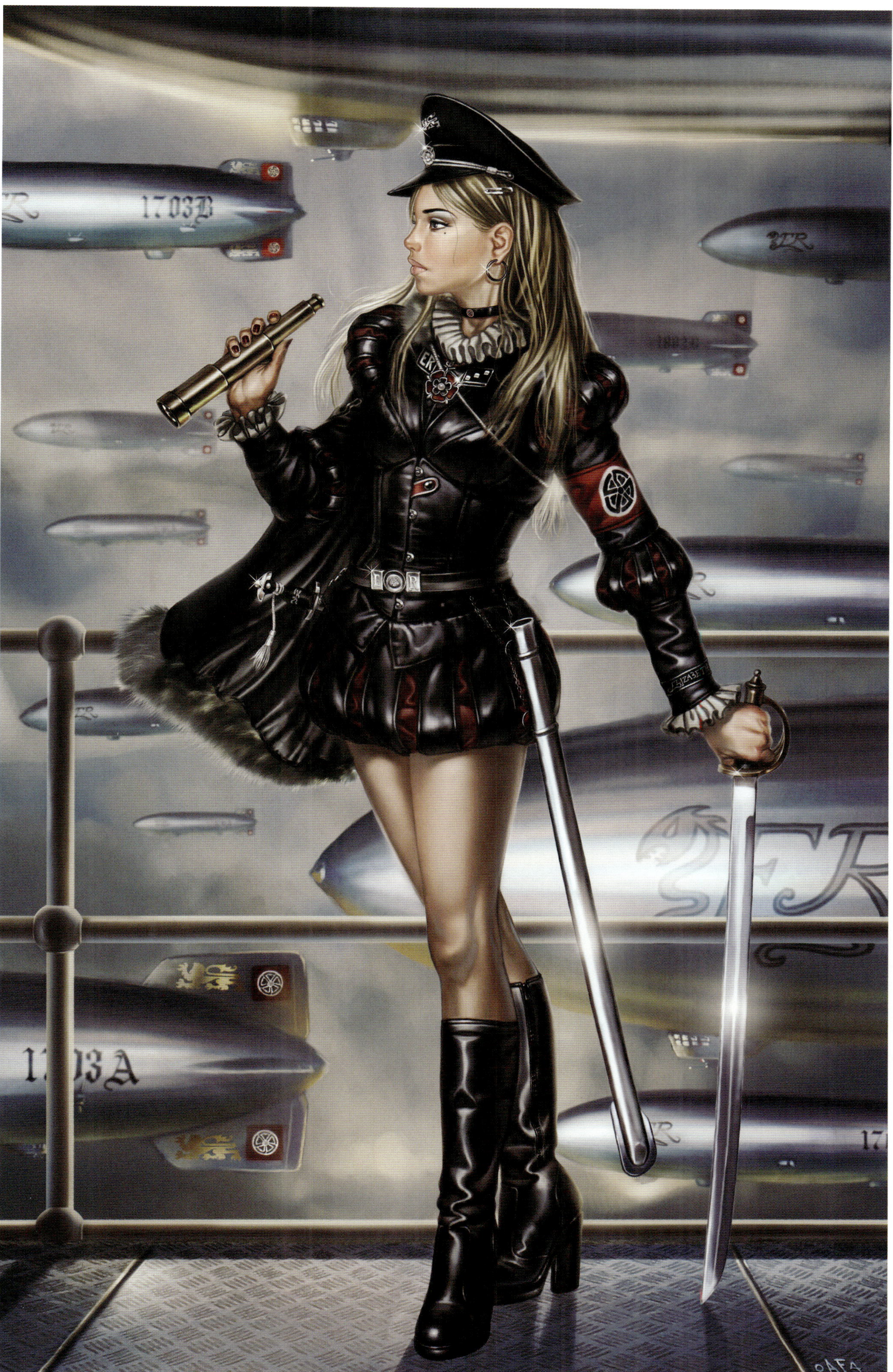

Lady Frances Drake

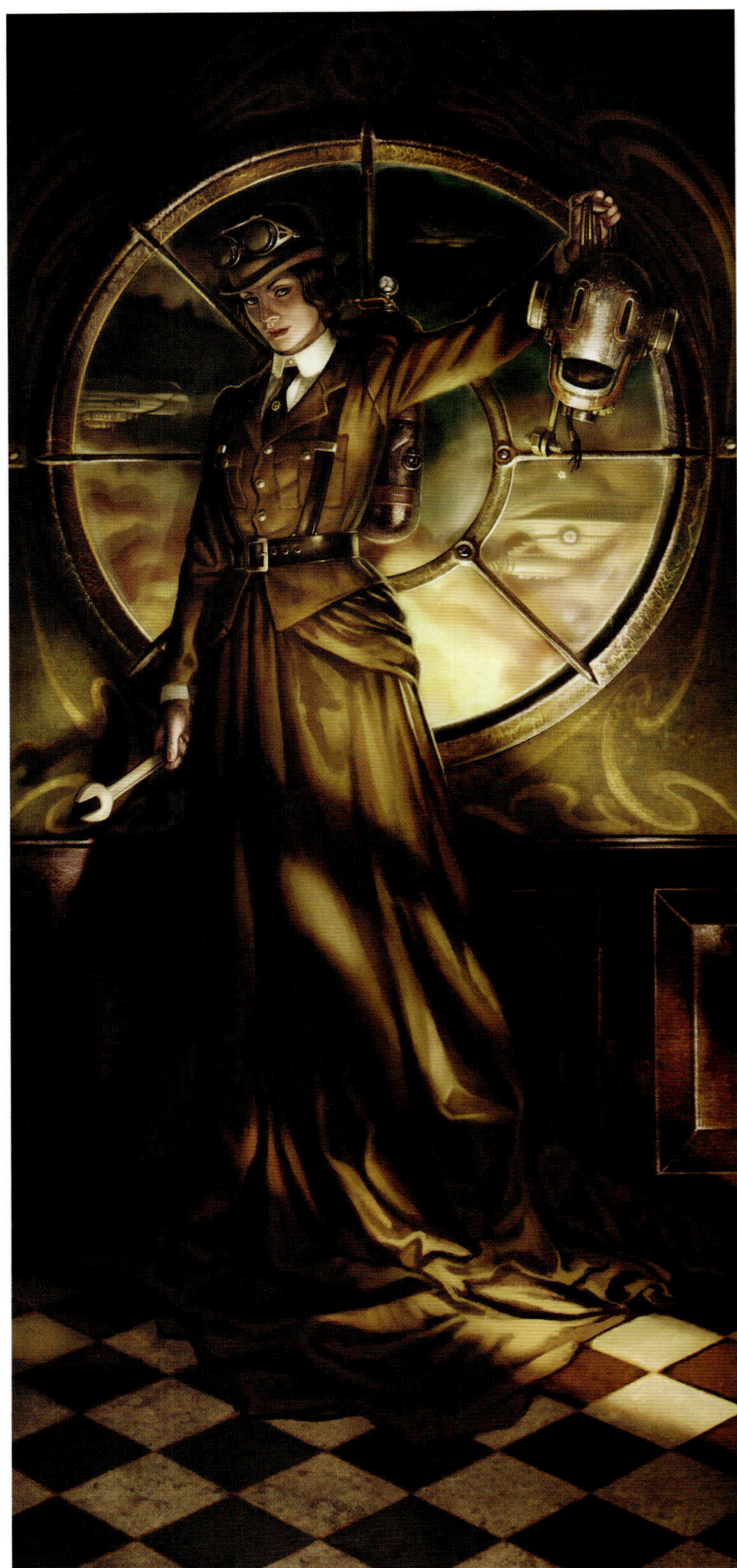

Judith and Holofernes

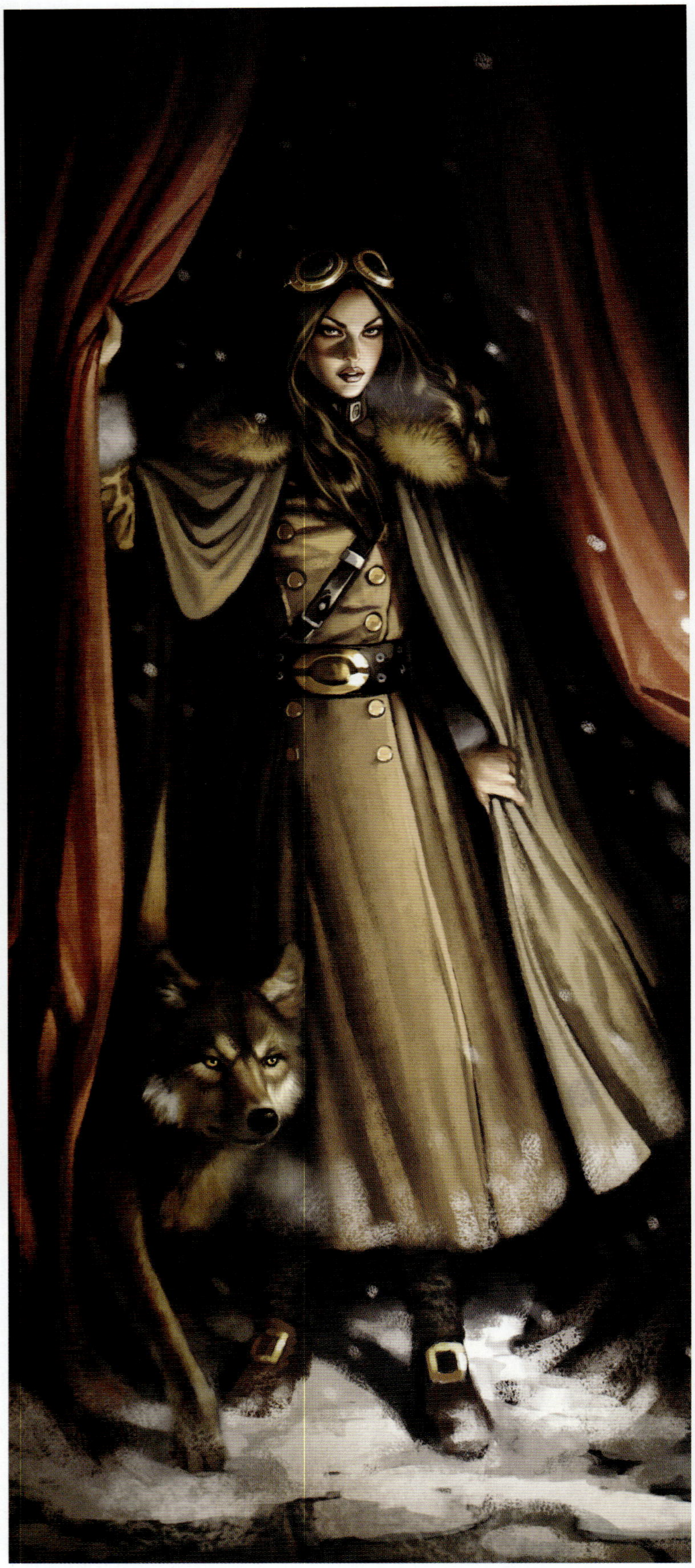

The Ice Princess

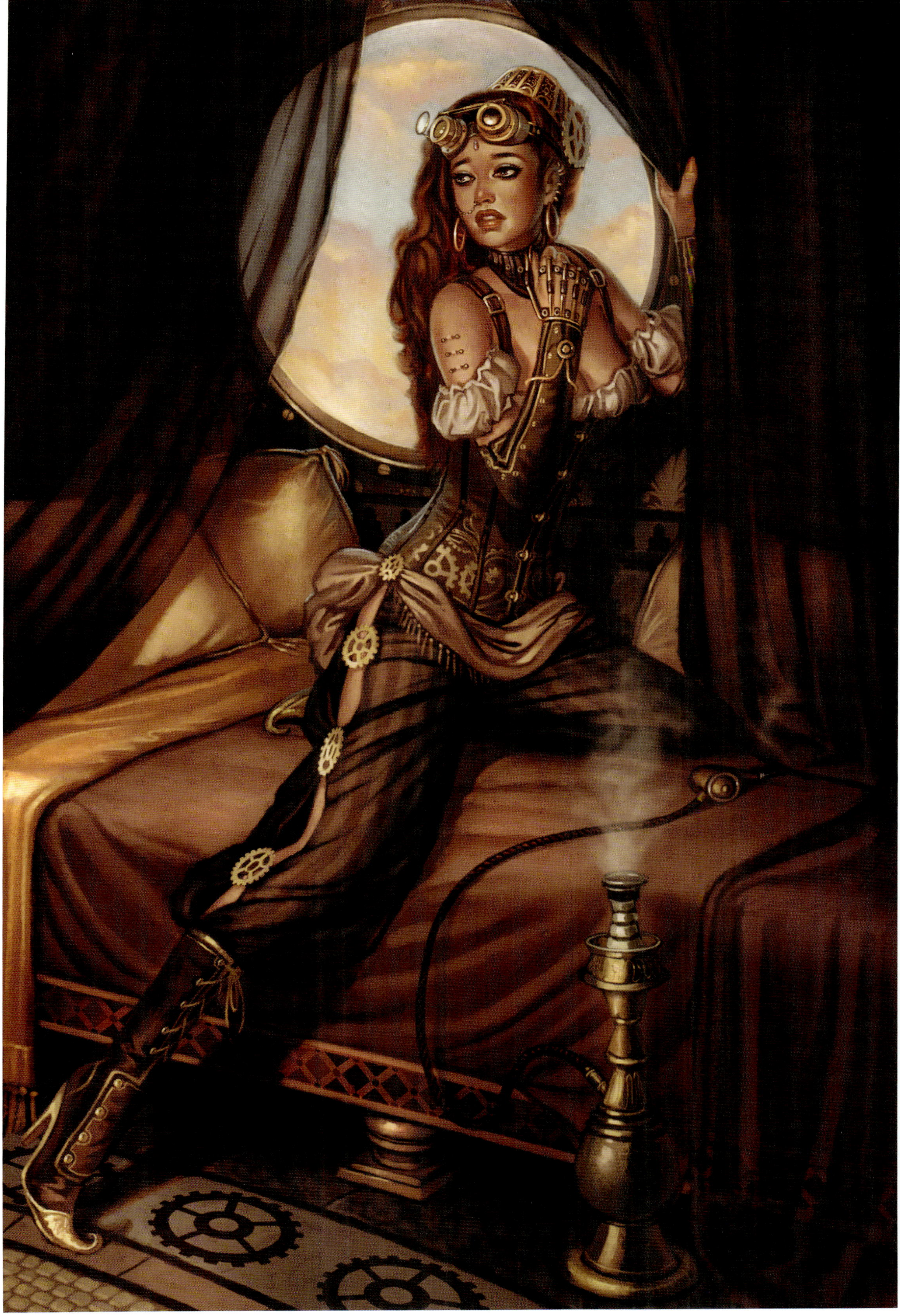

The Steampunk Harem

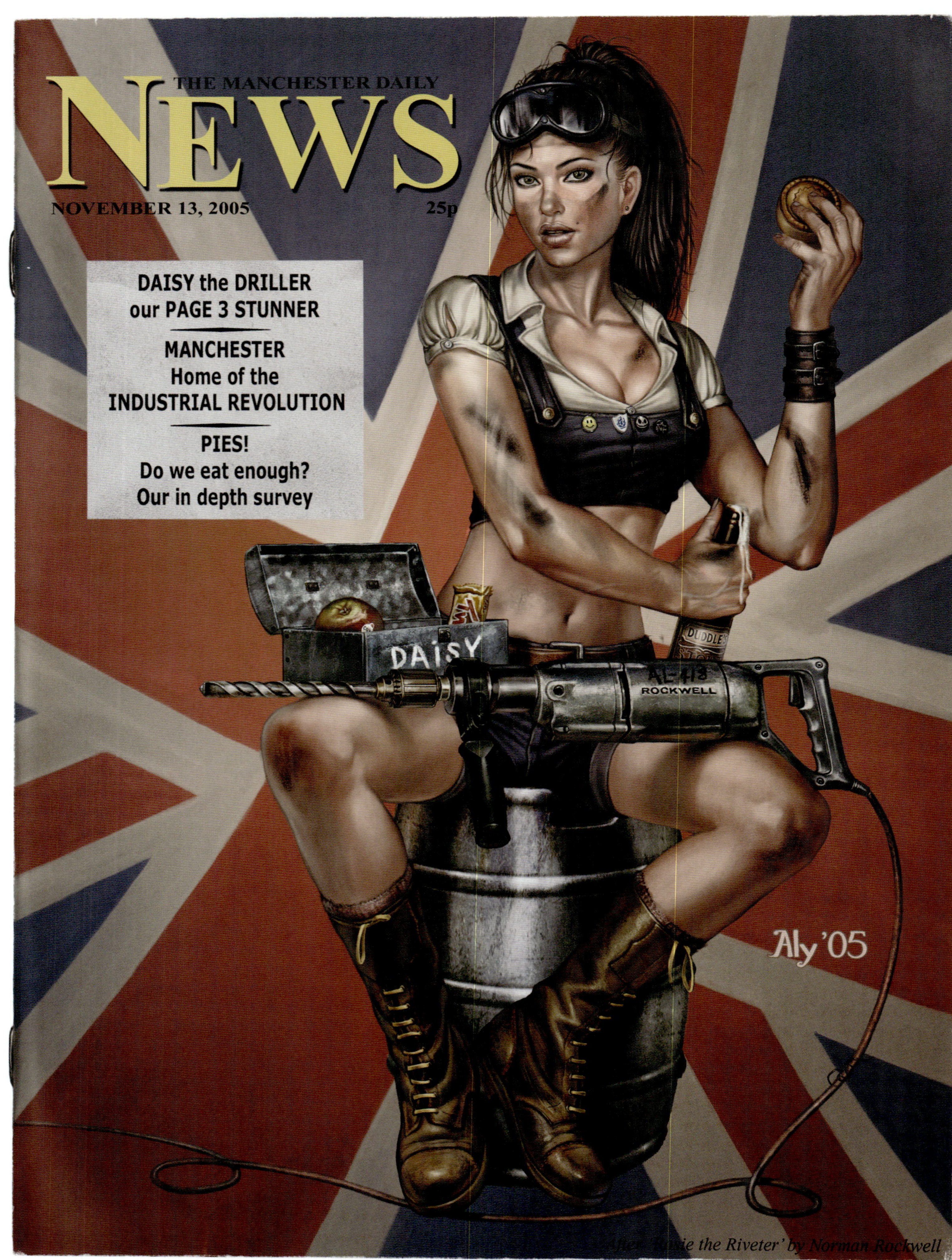

Daisy the Driller

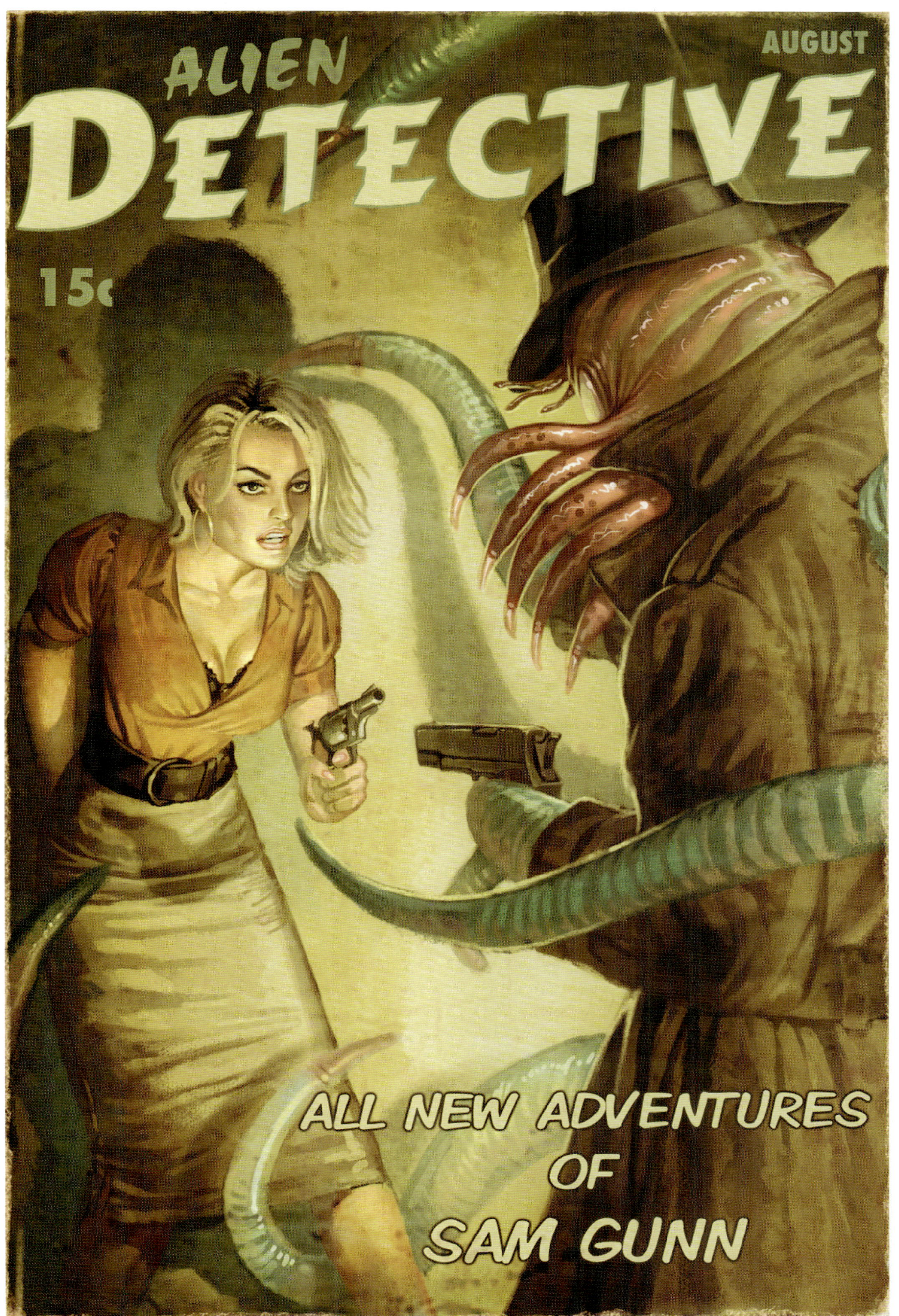

Alien Detective

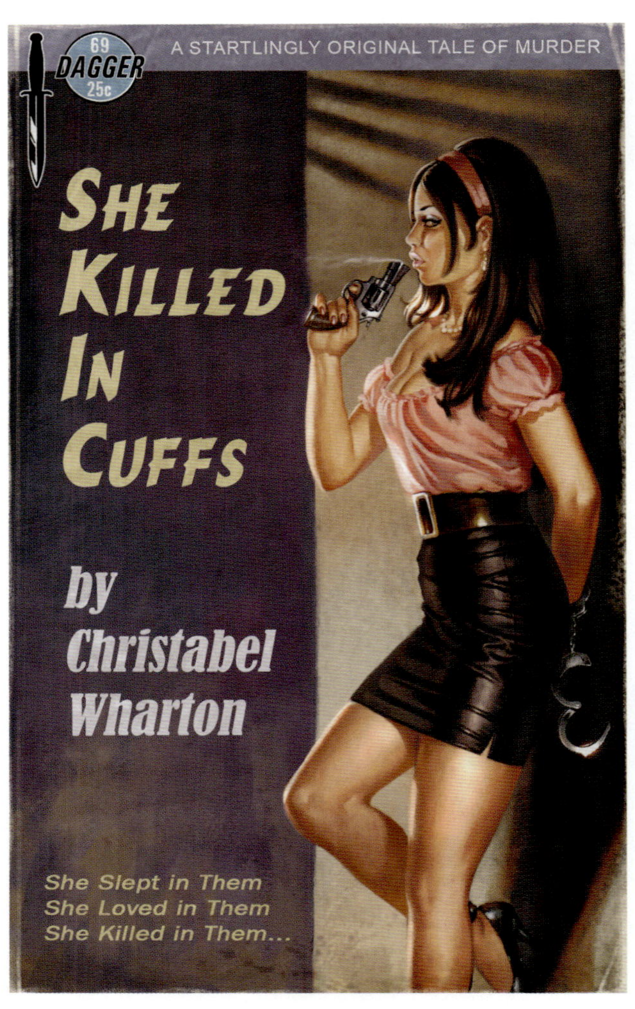

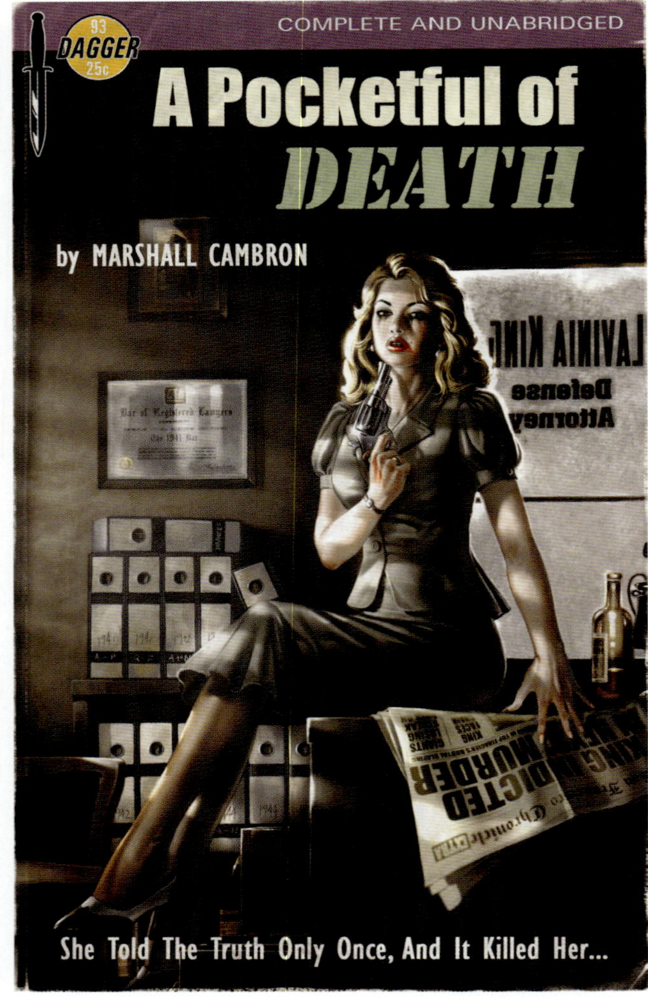

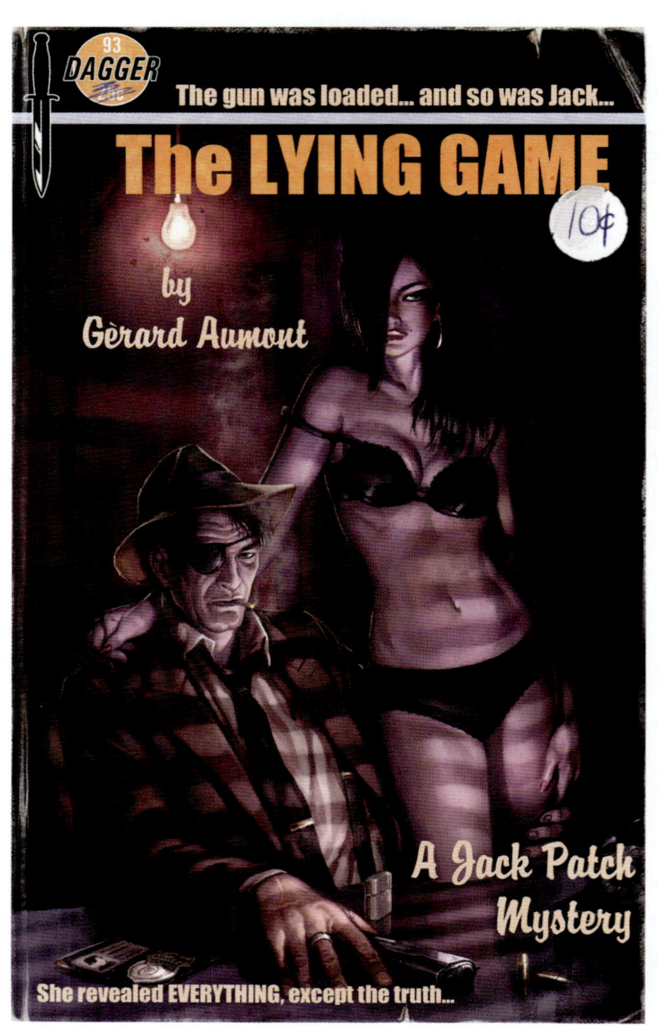

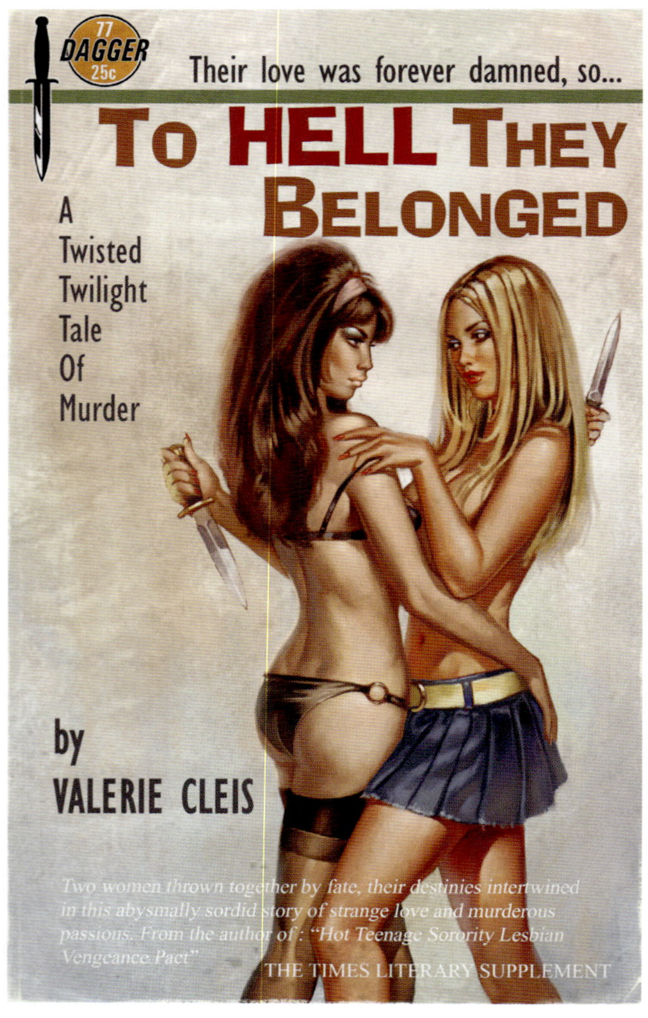

Pastiche Pulp Covers

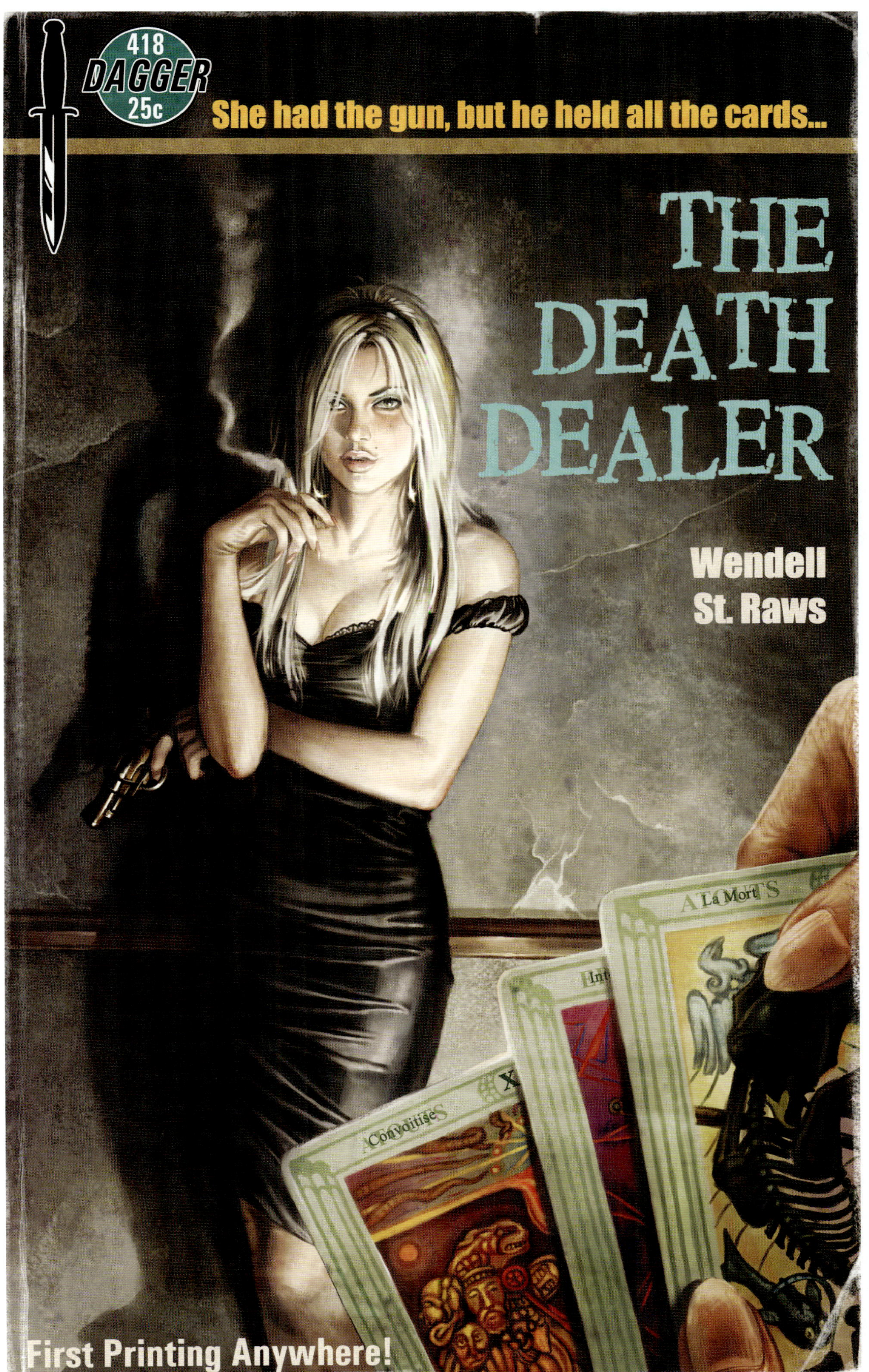

The Death Dealer

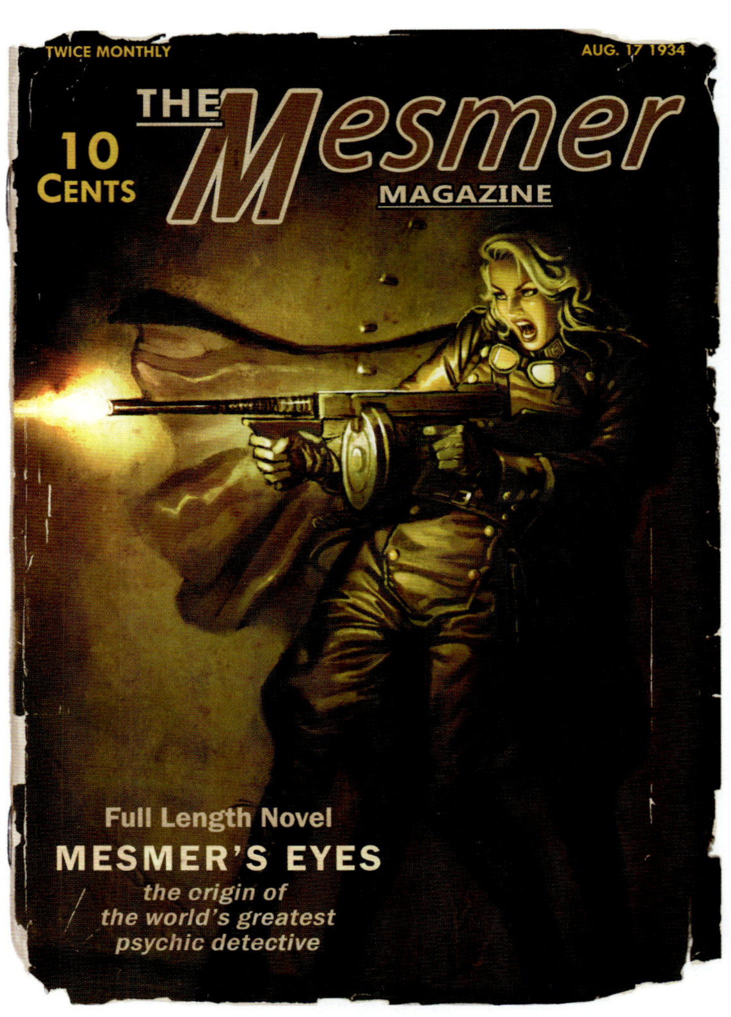

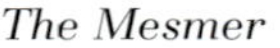

The Mesmer

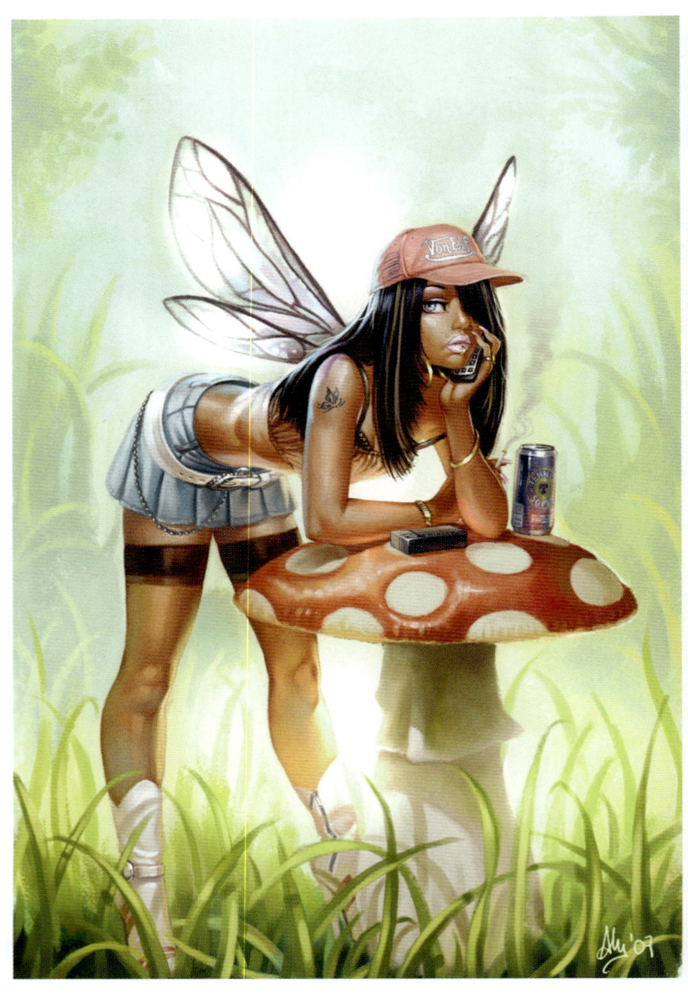

Fairies are Chavs

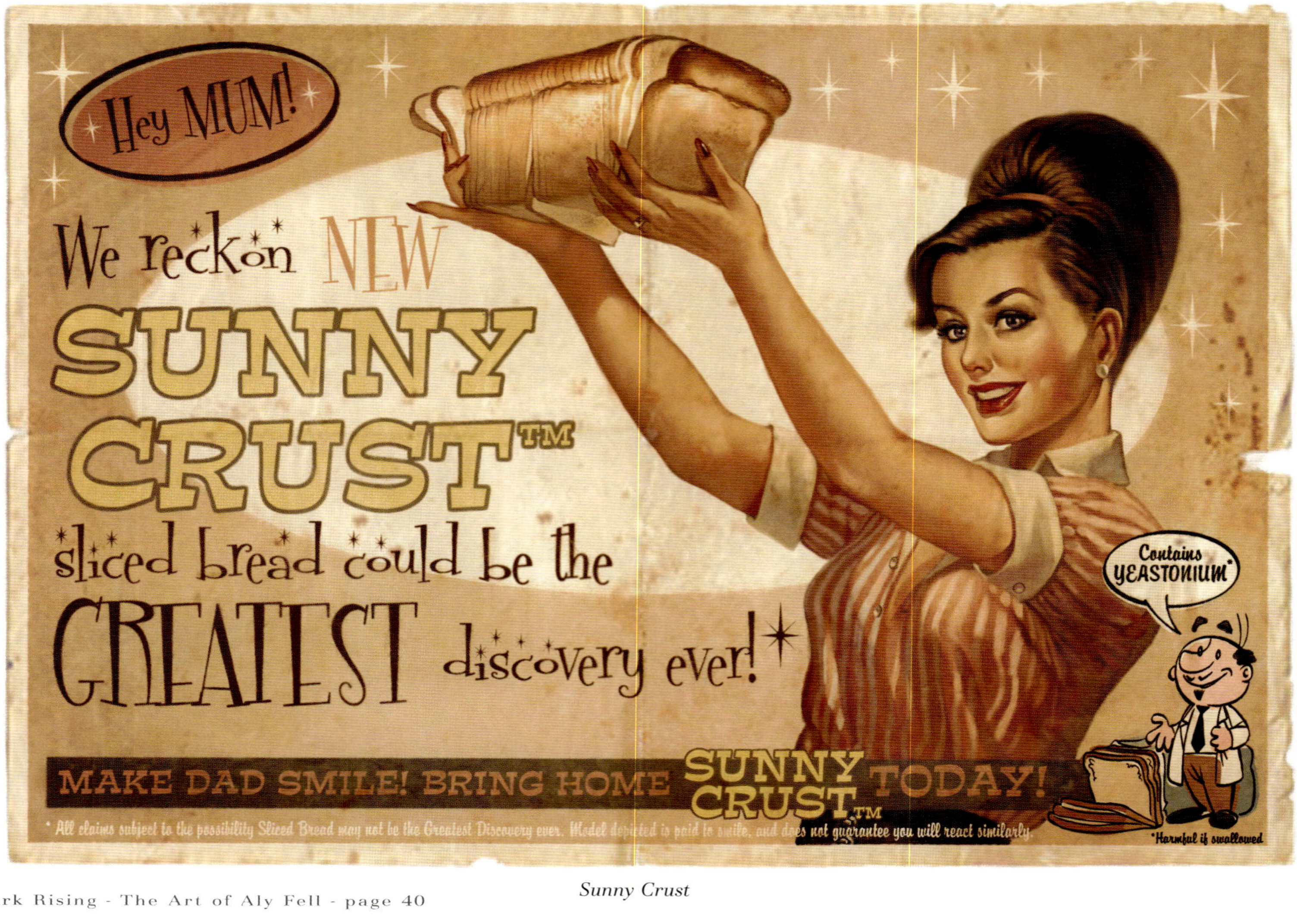

Sunny Crust

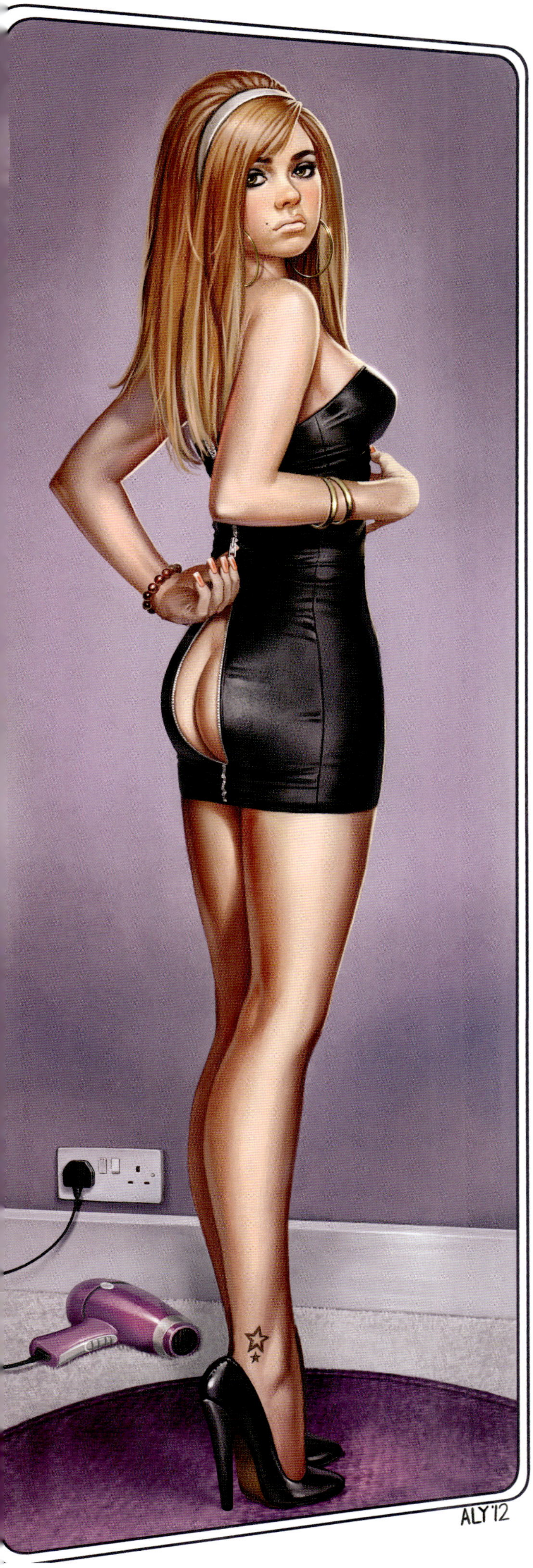

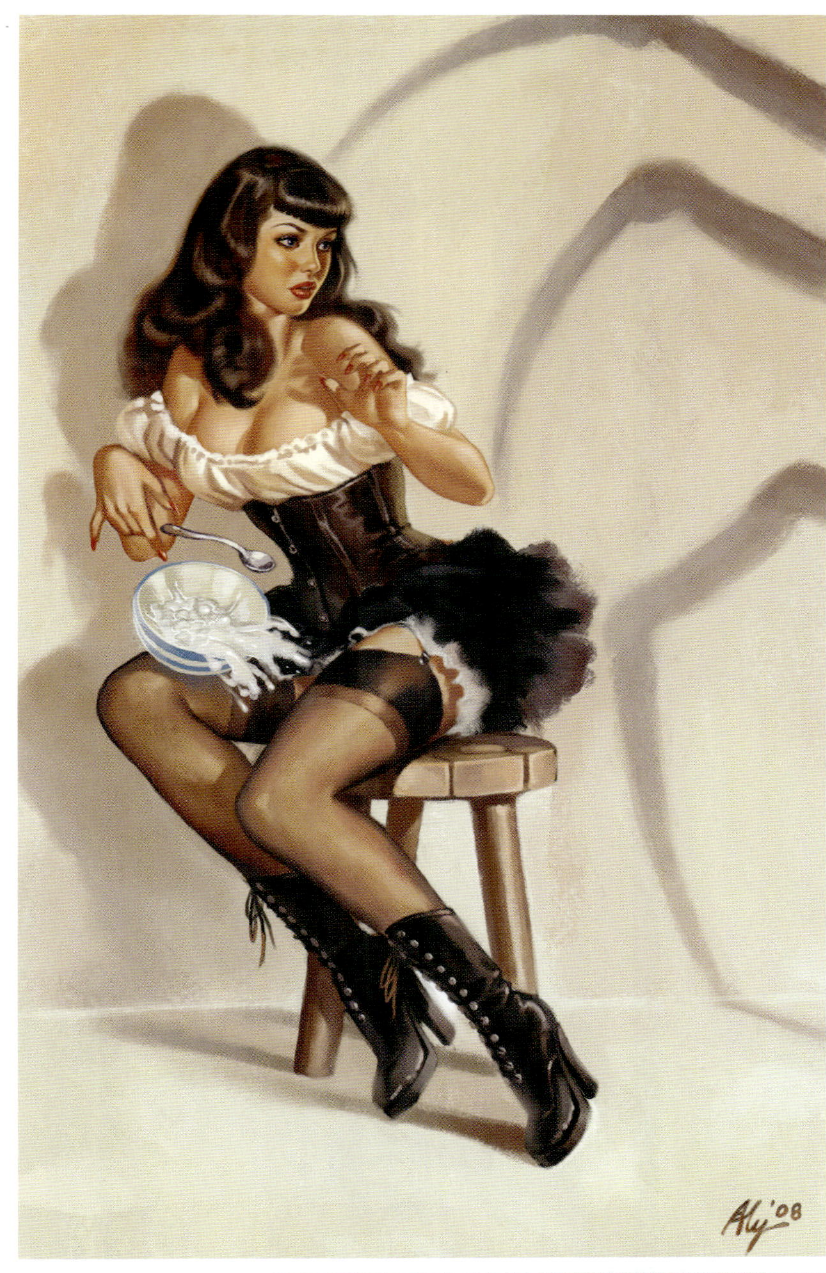

Clockwise from Left:

Tina's Broken Zip

Little Miss Muffet

Pierced Nipples

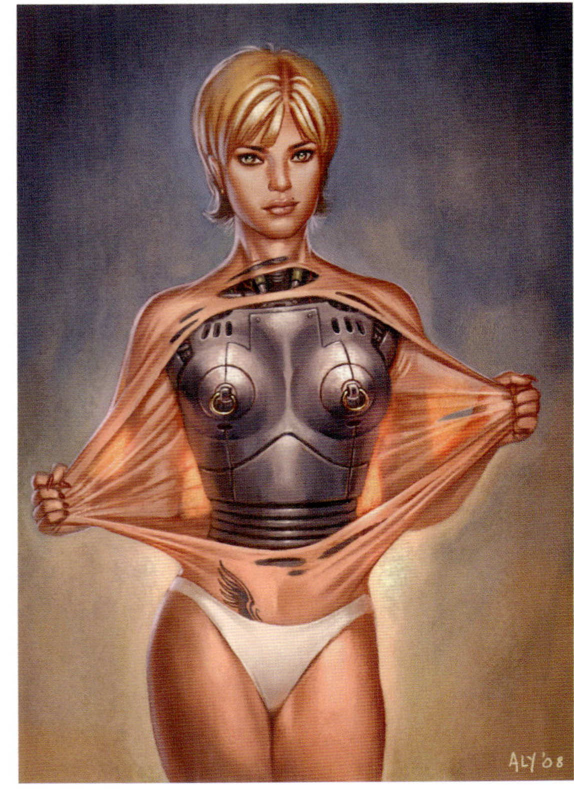

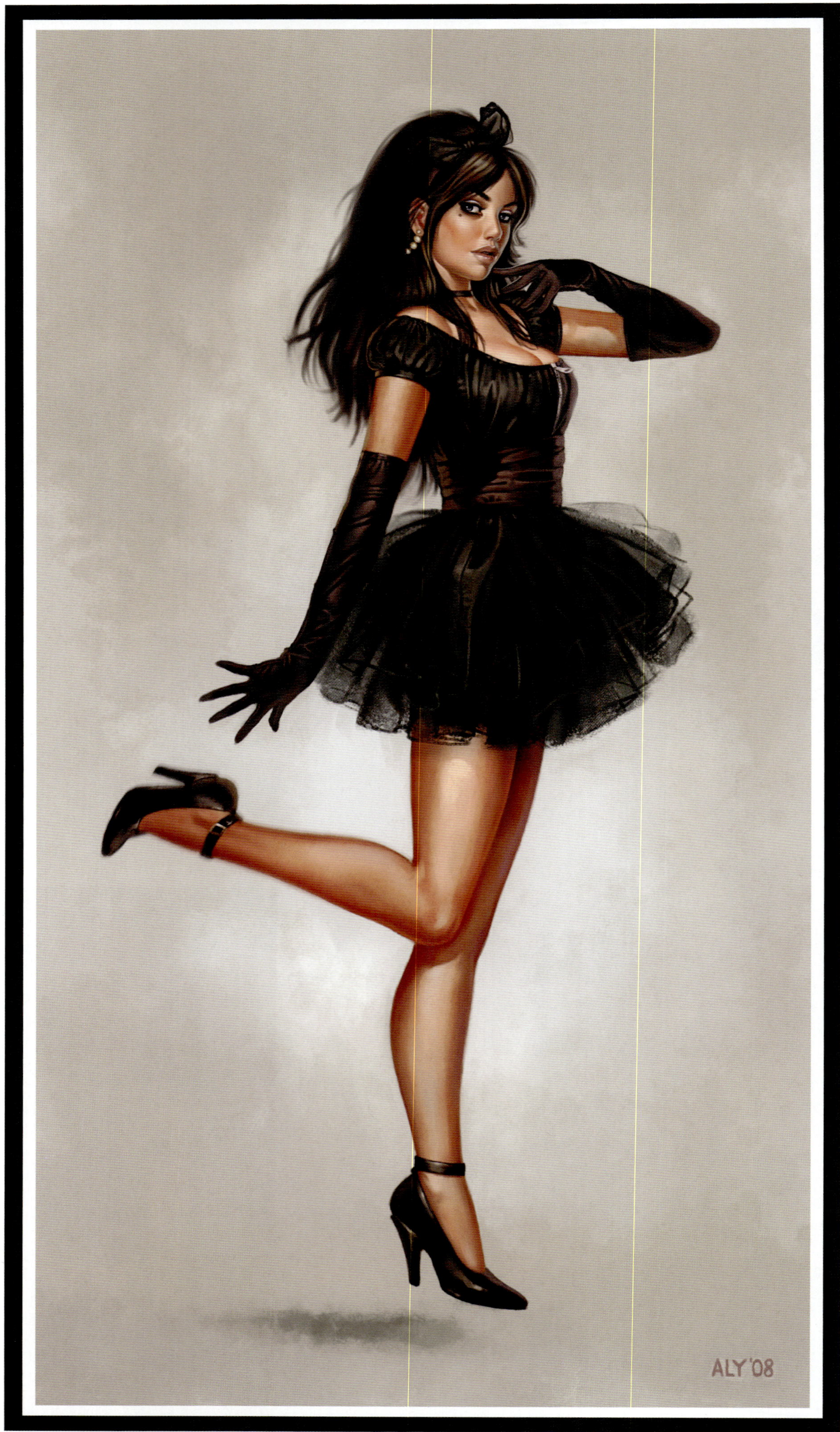

Bounce

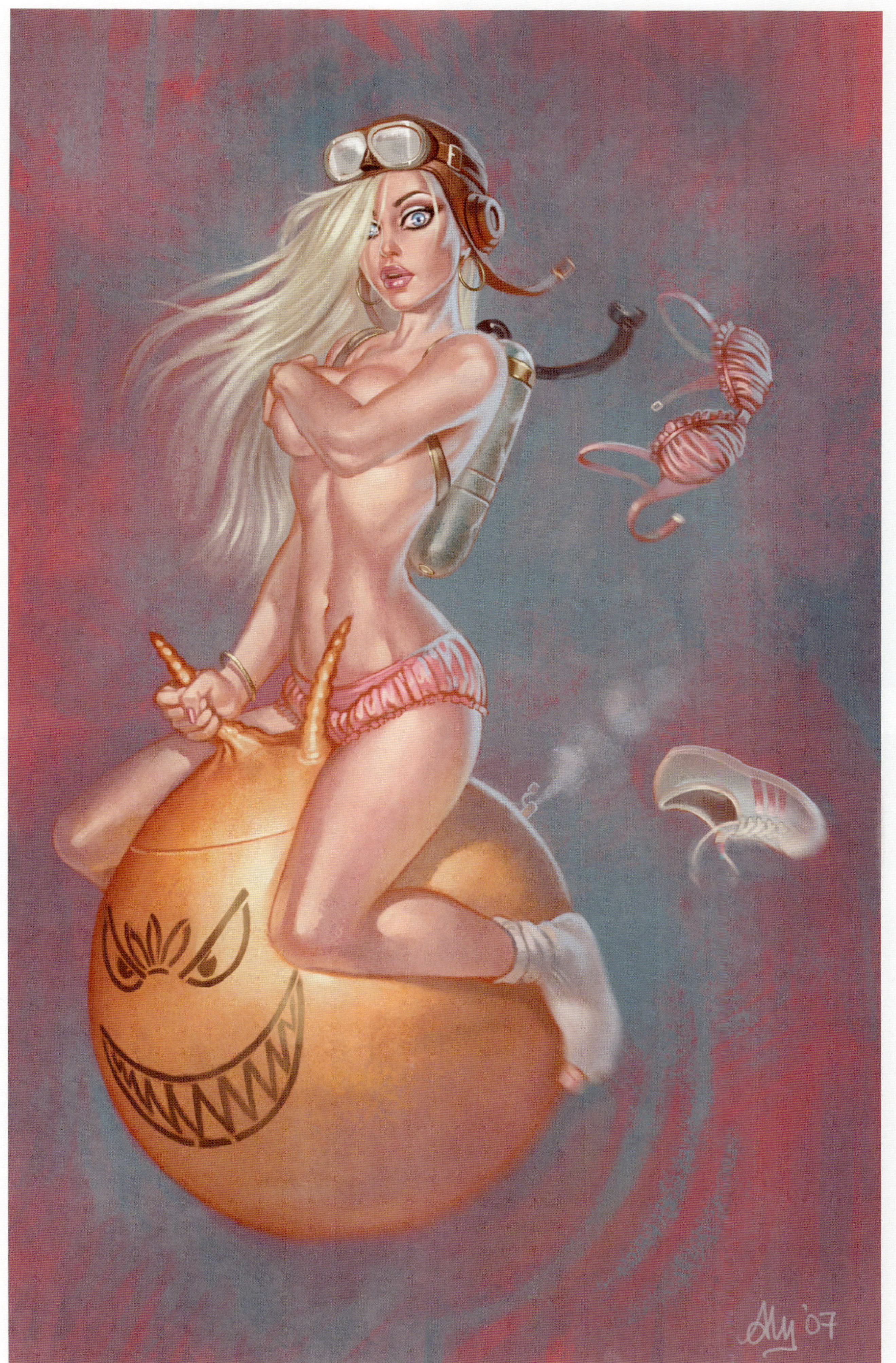

Boing!

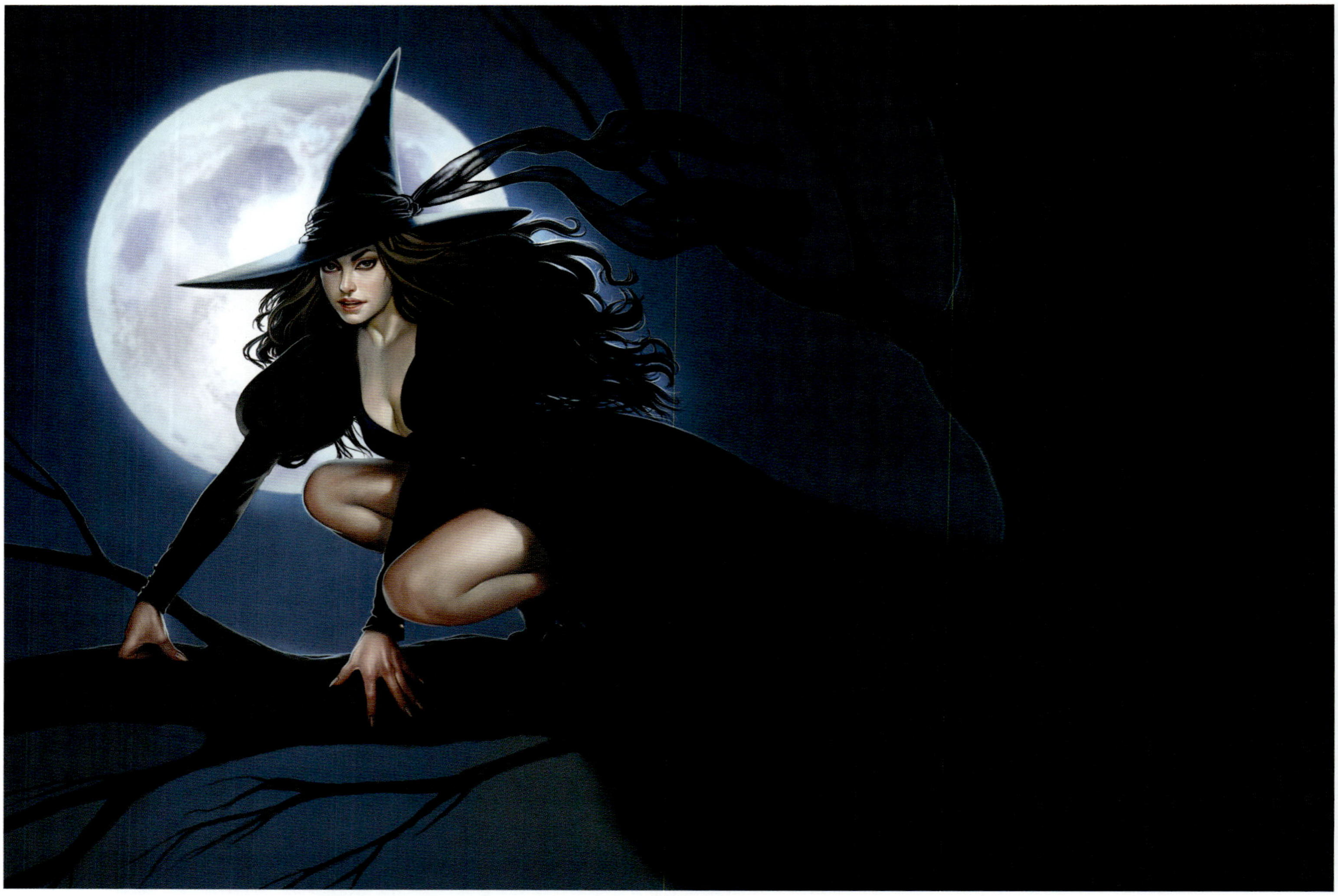

Hallowe'en Witch

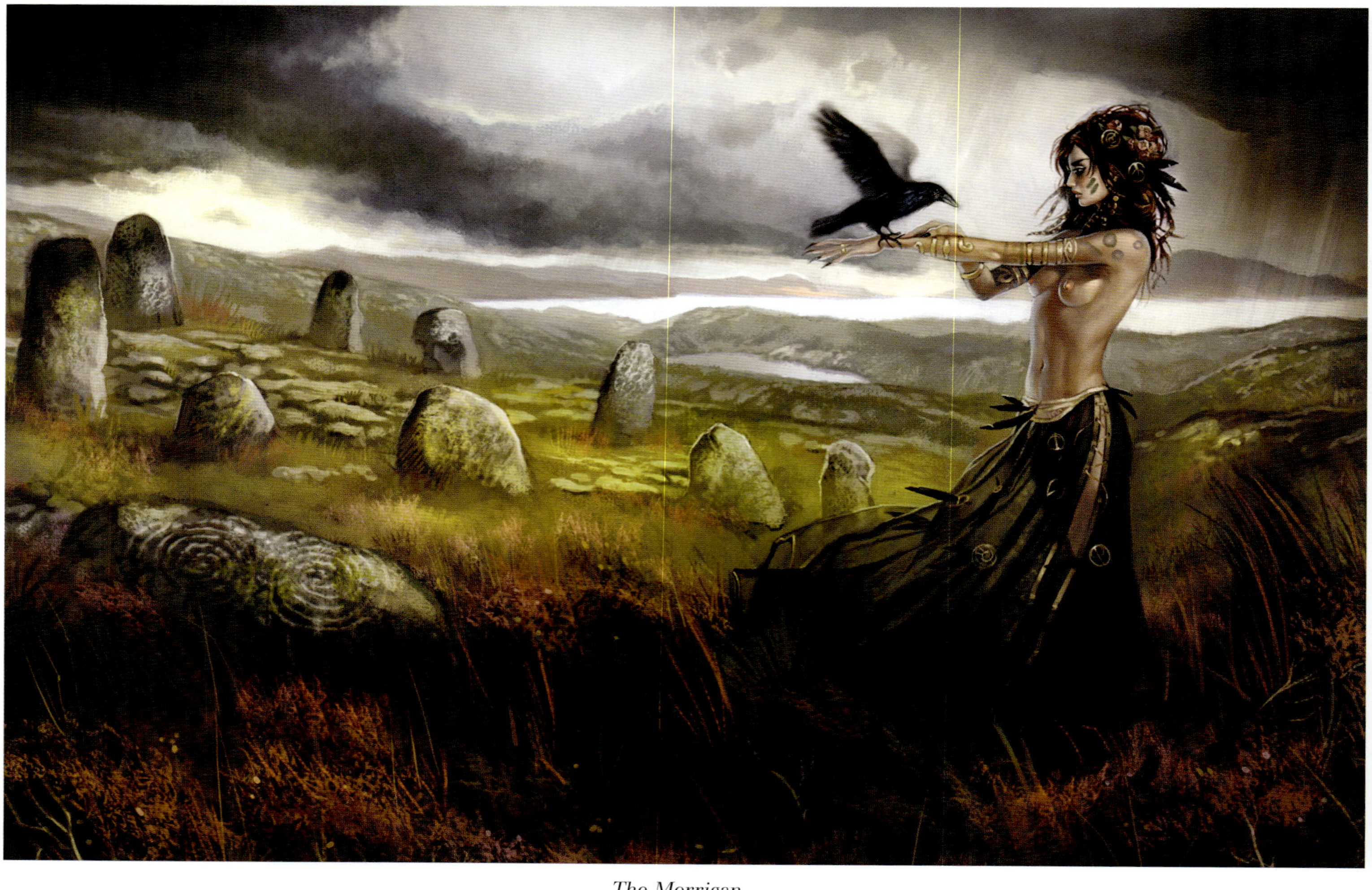

The Morrigan

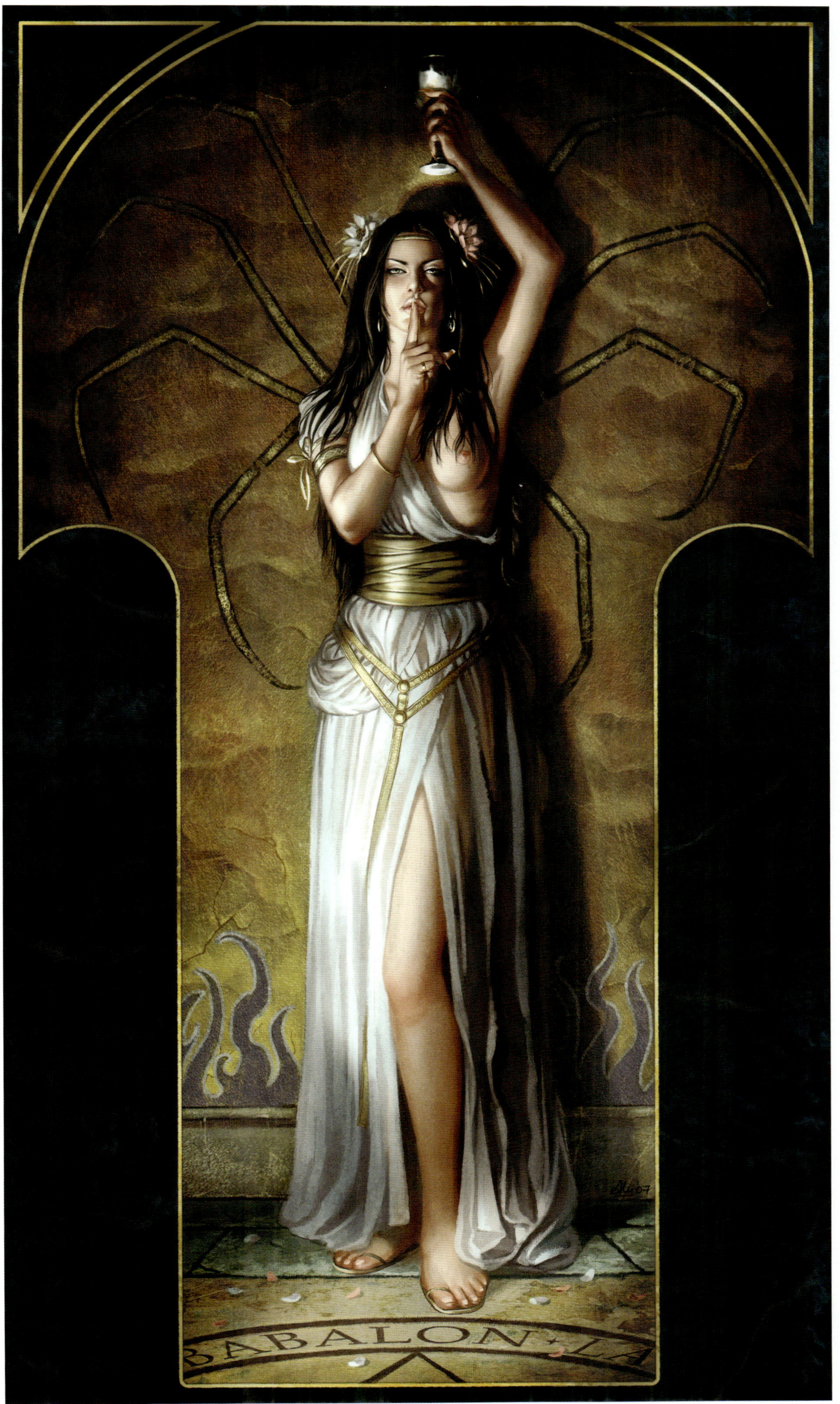

The Chalice

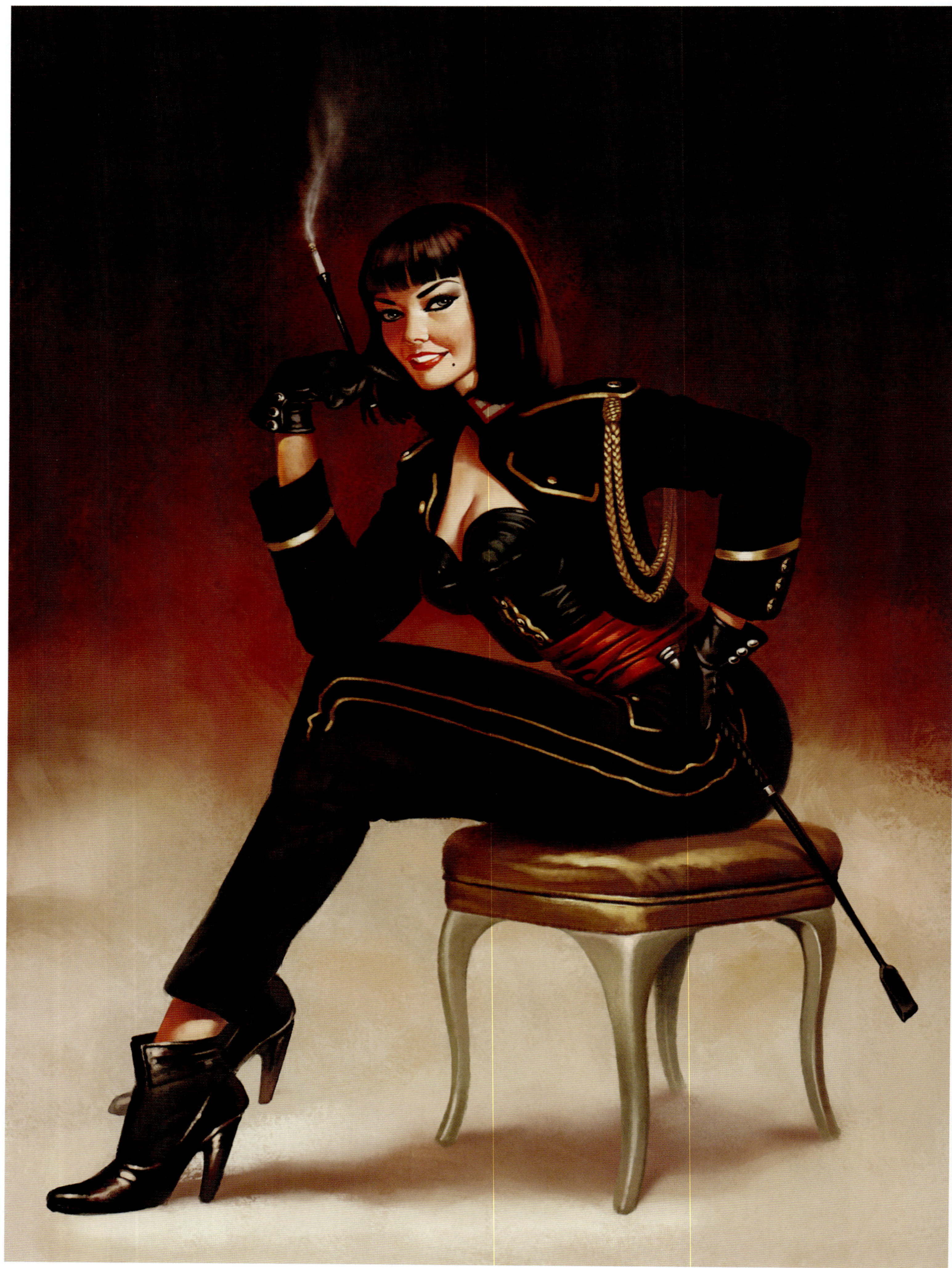

Silhouette

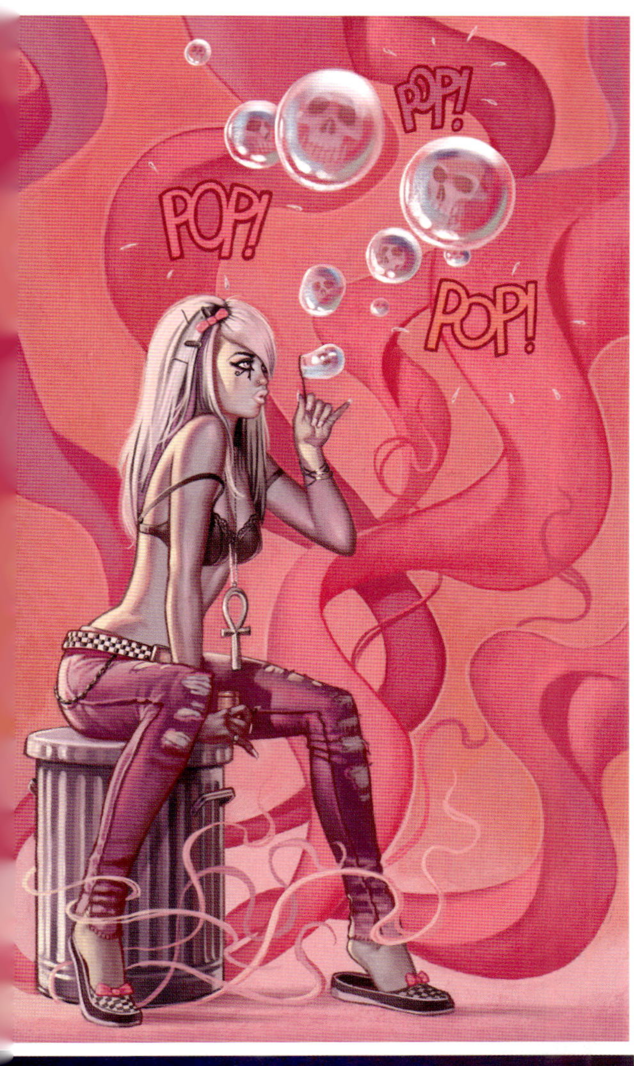

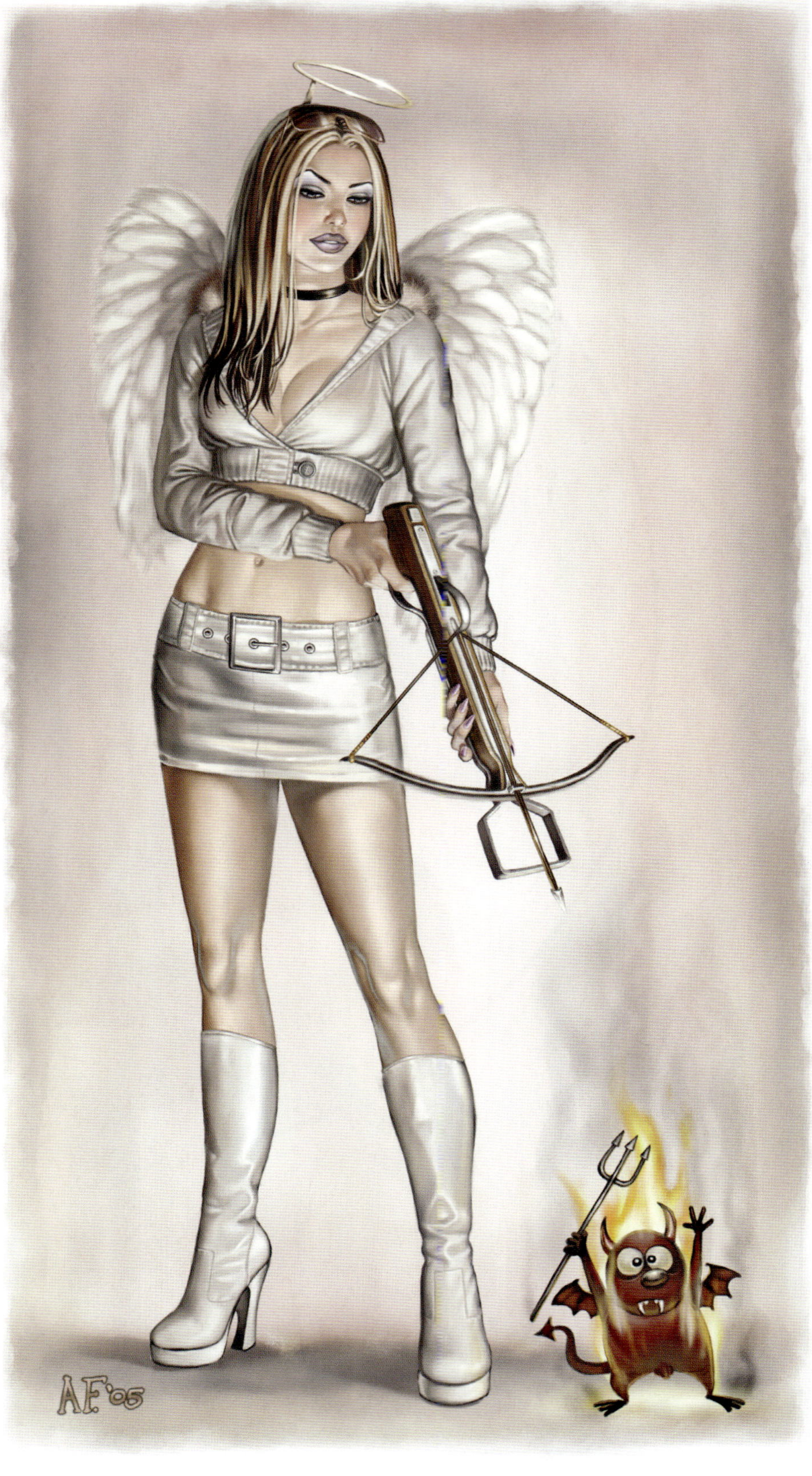

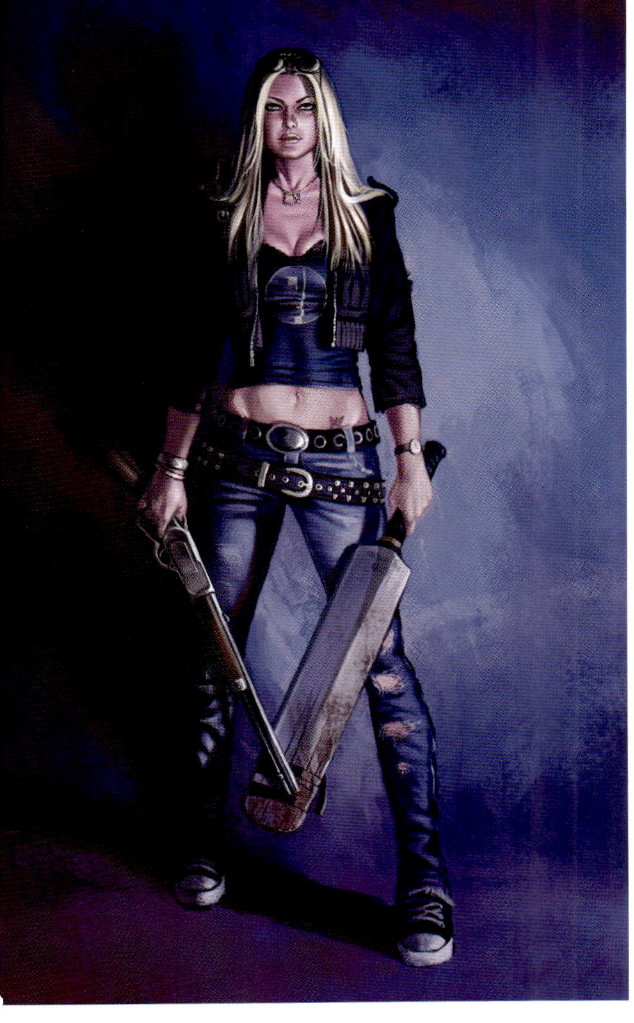

Clockwise from Upper Left:

Death Goes Emo

Hands Up

Erica: Zombie Slayer

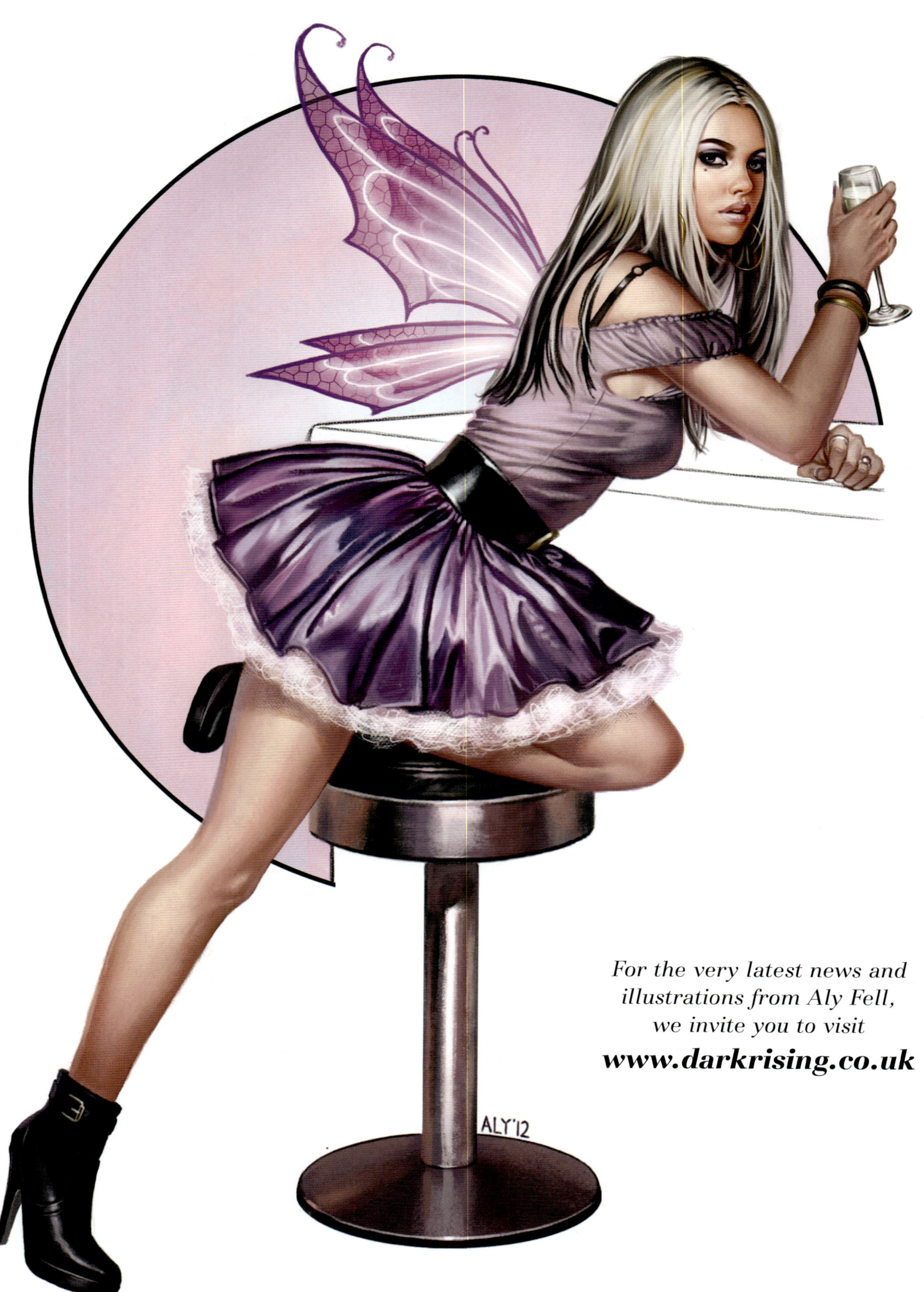

Bar Fairy

For the very latest news and illustrations from Aly Fell, we invite you to visit

www.darkrising.co.uk